ILTS

Middle Grades Mathematics Practice Questions

Mometrix
TEST PREPARATION

DEAR FUTURE EXAM SUCCESS STORY

First of all, **THANK YOU** for purchasing Mometrix study materials!

Second, congratulations! You are one of the few determined test-takers who are committed to doing whatever it takes to excel on your exam. **You have come to the right place.** We developed these practice tests with one goal in mind: to deliver you the best possible approximation of the questions you will see on test day.

Standardized testing is one of the biggest obstacles on your road to success, which only increases the importance of doing well in the high-pressure, high-stakes environment of test day. Your results on this test could have a significant impact on your future, and these practice tests will give you the repetitions you need to build your familiarity and confidence with the test content and format to help you achieve your full potential on test day.

Your success is our success

We would love to hear from you! If you would like to share the story of your exam success or if you have any questions or comments in regard to our products, please contact us at **800-673-8175** or **support@mometrix.com**.

Thanks again for your business and we wish you continued success!

Sincerely,
The Mometrix Test Preparation Team

Printed in the United States of America

Table of Contents

Practice Test #1

Multiple Choice

1. Which of the following represents the net of a square pyramid?

a. 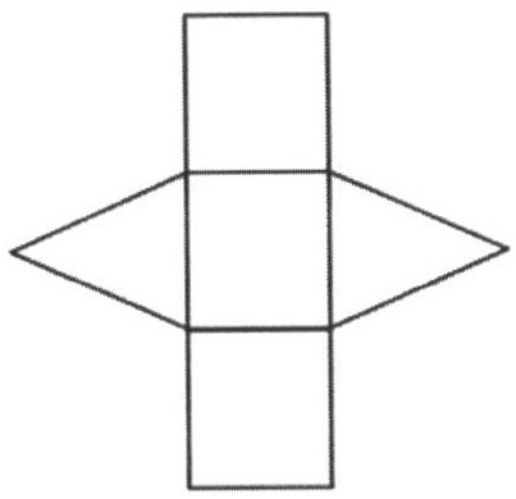

b. 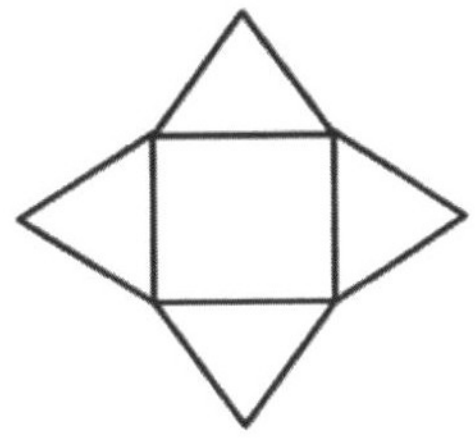

c. 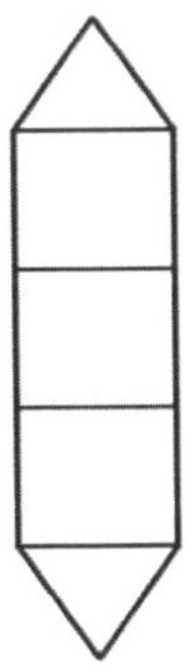

d. 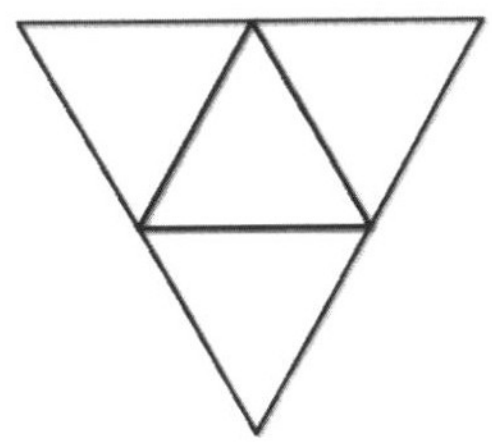

2. A man standing on a flat, level surface casts a shadow that is 6.2 ft in length. The man is 5.8 ft tall. Which of the following best represents the distance from the top of his head to the end of the shadow?

a. 7 ft
b. 7.5 ft
c. 8 ft
d. 8.5 ft

3. A dress is marked down 45%. The cost, after taxes, is $39.95. If the tax rate is 8.75%, what was the original price of the dress?

a. $45.74
b. $58.61
c. $66.79
d. $72.31

4. What is the size of the sample space for tossing four coins?

a. 8
b. 12
c. 16
d. 20

5. A coin is tossed three times. What is the size of the resulting sample space?

a. 8
b. 12
c. 16
d. 20

6. A fifth-grade teacher assigns her students a new math problem to be solved by the end of the day. Which of these is the most effective method of assessing students' work?

a. Administering a standardized test
b. Classroom observation
c. Portfolio assessment
d. Small group discussion

7. Which of the following describes a sampling technique that will likely increase the sampling error?

a. Choosing every 4th person from a list
b. Decreasing the sample size
c. Grouping a sample according to age and then choosing every 7th person from the list
d. Assigning numbers to a sample and then using a random number generator to choose numbers

8. Which of the following equations represents a line perpendicular to the one graphed below and passing through the point $(1, -2)$?

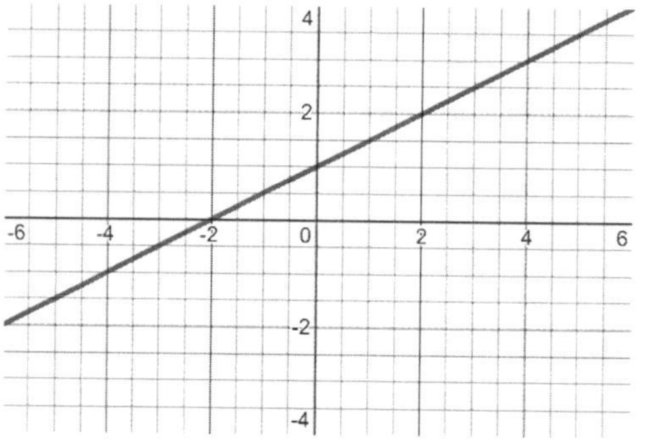

a. $y = \frac{1}{2}x + 1$
b. $y = \frac{1}{2}x - 1$
c. $y = -2x + \frac{1}{2}$
d. $y = -2x$

9. Nikki buys a used book that is marked down 35% from the original price. She pays 8.25% sales tax. Her total cost is \$9.14. What was the original price of the book?

a. \$11.99
b. \$12.49
c. \$12.99
d. \$13.49

10. 320 students are surveyed. 120 of the students like only Dallas. 150 of the students like only Houston. 48 of the students like neither city. How many students like Dallas *and* Houston?

a. 2
b. 3
c. 4
d. 5

11. The variables x and y are in a linear relationship. The table below shows a few sample values. Which of the following graphs correctly represents the linear equation relating x and y?

x	y
−2	2
−1	1.5
0	1
1	0.5
2	0

a. 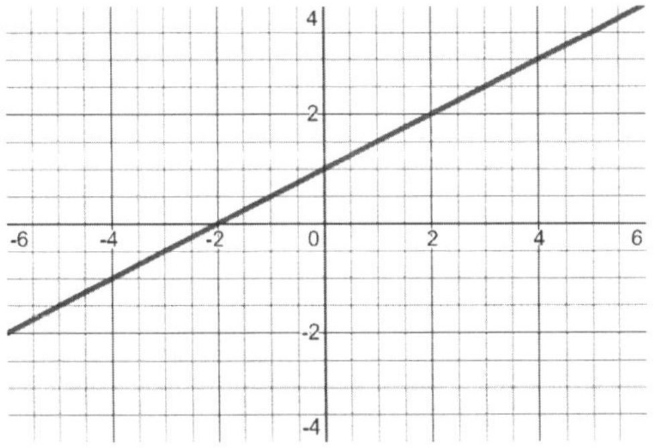

b. 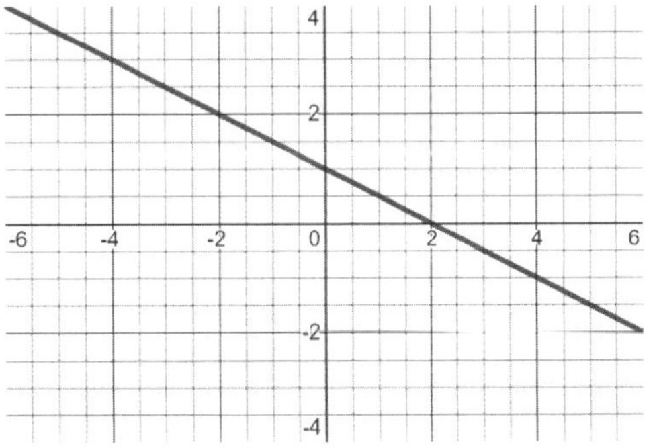

c. 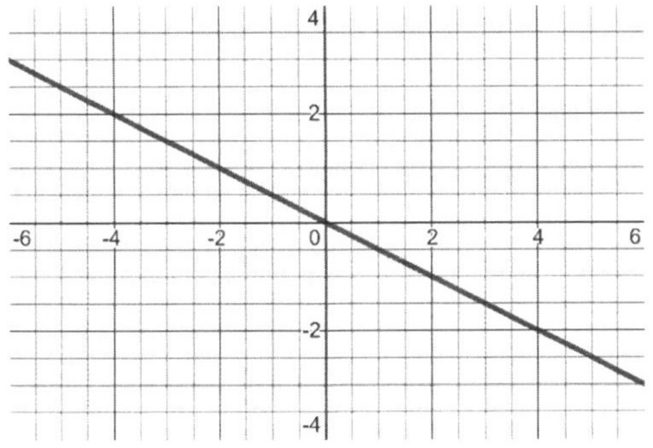

d. 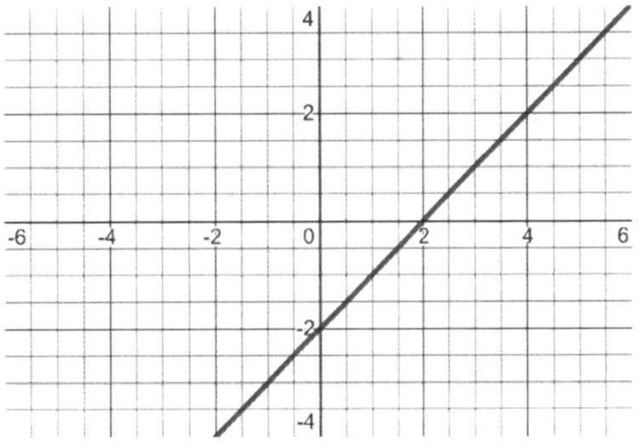

12. Which of the following activities would students be able to complete successfully BEFORE they can identify the relationship between counting and the concept of larger and smaller numbers?

a. Assign the correct number to a group of objects.
b. Choose which of two groups of objects contains more, is greater, or is larger.
c. Both (a) and (b)
d. Neither (a) nor (b)

13. Which of the following word problems is worded best to help students apply the distributive property?

a. Mikey is counting his art supplies. He has 2 boxes of crayons with 12 crayons in each box, 5 glue sticks, 3 sets of markers with 8 markers in each set, and one case of colored pencils that contains 16 pencils. Excluding the pencil box, how many items does Mikey have altogether?
b. Mikey is counting his art supplies. He has 2 pencil boxes. Each pencil box has 5 colored pencils and 8 markers. How many items does Mikey have altogether?
c. Mikey is counting his art supplies. He has 2 pencil boxes. Each pencil box has 5 colored pencils and 8 markers. How many markers does Mikey have? How many colored pencils does he have?
d. Mikey is counting his art supplies. He has 2 boxes of crayons with 12 crayons in each box, 5 glue sticks, 3 sets of markers with 8 markers in each set, and one case of colored pencils that contains 16 pencils. How many crayons does Mikey have?

14. Kyra sets aside $\frac{1}{3}$ of her income to pay rent and utilities at her apartment. If the monthly cost of rent and utilities is $1,050, what is her monthly salary?

a. $3,150
b. $3,225
c. $3,750
d. $4,050

15. What is the constant of proportionality represented by the table below?

x	y
−10	−5
−6	−3
−2	−1
0	0
4	2

a. -2
b. $-\frac{1}{2}$
c. 2
d. $\frac{1}{2}$

16. Which of the following is an irrational number?

a. $3.\overline{13}$
b. $\sqrt{25}$
c. $\frac{\pi}{2}$
d. $\frac{37}{5}$

17. The expression $5x^2 - 3x - 14$ is equal to the product of $(x - 2)$ and which other factor?

a. $(5x - 14)$
b. $(5x - 3)$
c. $(5x + 7)$
d. $(5x + 14)$

18. Before the start of the school year, a seventh-grade math teacher plans out how much time she will spend on each unit during the school year. She considers the English Language Development (ELD) standards that will be covered along with each content standard. What is this approach known as?

a. Backwards lesson planning
b. Differentiating lessons
c. Curriculum mapping
d. Holistic assessments

19. Given the diagram below, which of the following theorems may be used to verify that lines *a* and *b* are parallel?

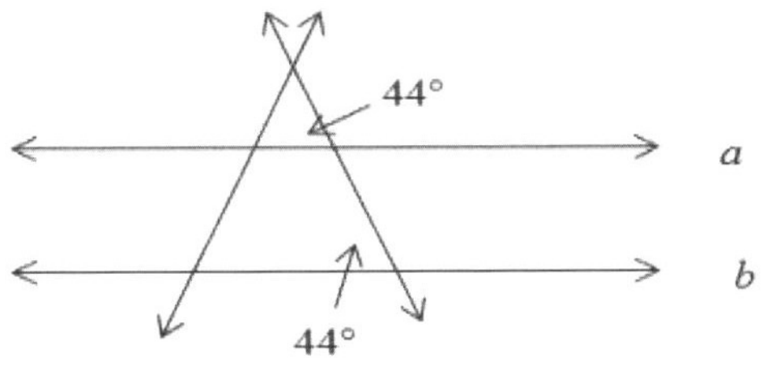

a. Alternate Interior Angles Converse Theorem
b. Alternate Exterior Angles Converse Theorem
c. Consecutive Interior Angles Converse Theorem
d. Corresponding Angles Converse Theorem

20. What is the constant of proportionality represented by the table below?

x	y
2	−8
5	−20
7	−28
10	−40
11	−44

a. −12
b. −8
c. −6
d. −4

21. Which of the following represents an inversely proportional relationship?

a. $y = 3x$
b. $y = \frac{1}{3}x$
c. $y = \frac{3}{x}$
d. $y = 3x^2$

22. What is the sum of the first 35 odd, positive integers?

a. 1,225
b. 1,435
c. 1,850
d. 2,250

23. $f(x) = \frac{3x-5}{2x}$. **What is the equation of the horizontal asymptote?**

a. $y = -\frac{5}{2}$
b. $y = \frac{1}{2}$
c. $y = 0$
d. $y = \frac{3}{2}$

24. Which of the following best represents the measurement of x, shown in the right triangle below?

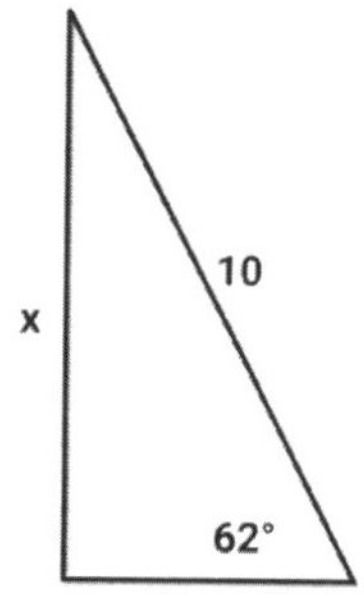

a. 5.6
b. 6.4
c. 7.9
d. 8.8

25. What is the solution to the system of linear equations below?

$$2x - 3y = 24$$
$$5x + 6y = -21$$

a. $(-6,3)$
b. $(-3,-10)$
c. $(3,-6)$
d. $(6,-4)$

26. The two prisms shown below are similar (units are inches). What is the measure of x?

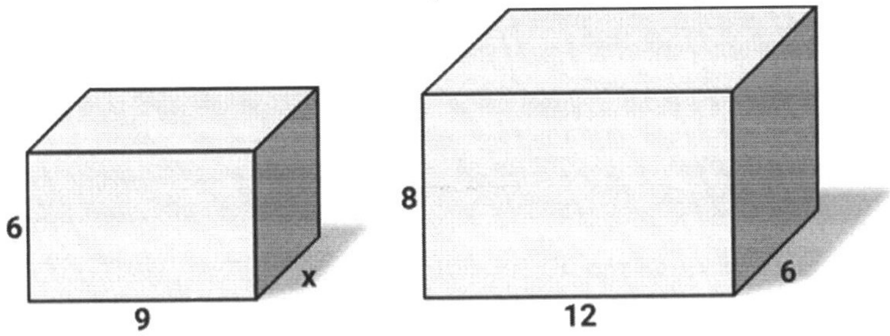

a. $4\frac{1}{2}$ in
b. $4\frac{3}{4}$ in
c. 5 in
d. $5\frac{1}{4}$ in

27. What is the contrapositive of the statement below?

If I get paid, then I go to the beach.

a. If I get paid, then I do not go to the beach.
b. If I go to the beach, then I get paid.
c. If I do not get paid, then I go to the beach.
d. If I do not go to the beach, then I do not get paid.

28. Which of the following correctly compares the sets of rational and irrational numbers?

a. The set of rational numbers is a subset of the set of irrational numbers.
b. The set of irrational numbers is a subset of the set of rational numbers.
c. The sets of irrational and rational numbers are disjoint.
d. The sets of irrational and rational numbers are equal.

29. What is the solution to the system of linear equations below?

$$4x - 2y = -38$$
$$2x + 3y = 17$$

a. $(-5,9)$
b. $(-2,11)$
c. $(-3,7)$
d. $(-4,11)$

30. Which of the following is an irrational number?

a. $4.\overline{2}$
b. $\sqrt{2}$
c. $\frac{4}{5}$
d. $\frac{21}{5}$

31. You wish to determine the area of a regular pentagon, and all you know is the length of one side. What additional information is sufficient for you to be able to compute the area?

a. The length of all the other sides
b. The width of the pentagon
c. The length of the apothem
d. No other information needed

32. What is the value of x, shown in the diagram below?

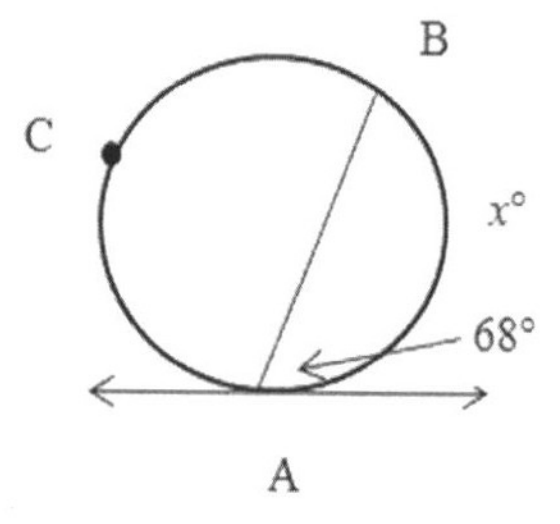

a. 68°
b. 76°
c. 128°
d. 136°

33. For how long at a time should a teacher initially plan to hold open class discussions of subject matter at the middle school/junior high school level?

a. 3-5 minutes
b. 10-15 minutes
c. 30-45 minutes
d. For an entire class period

34. Which of the following represents a discretionary expense?

a. Textbook
b. Rent
c. DVD
d. Groceries

35. Which of the following describes a sampling technique that will likely increase the sampling error?

a. choosing every 5th person from a list
b. grouping a sample according to gender and then choosing every 10th person from a list
c. using an intact group
d. assigning numbers to a sample and then using a random number generator to choose numbers

36. Given the diagram below, which of the following theorems may be used to verify that lines *a* and *b* are parallel?

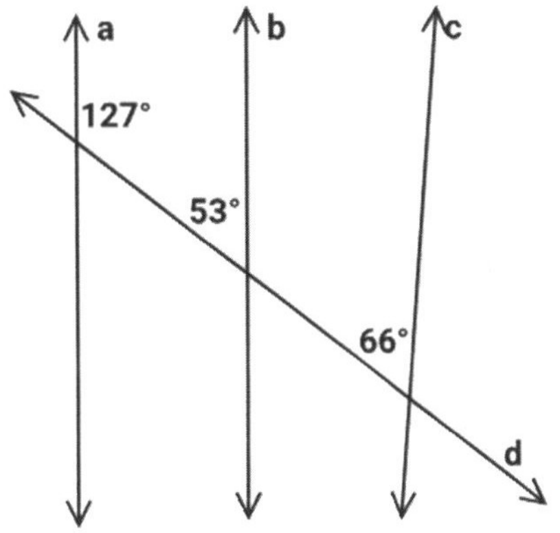

a. Alternate Interior Angles Converse Theorem
b. Alternate Exterior Angles Converse Theorem
c. Consecutive Interior Angles Converse Theorem
d. Corresponding Angles Converse Theorem

37. A teacher has concerns that a standardized test she is required to give does not accurately measure what it is designed to measure. The test claims to measure students' abilities to make inferences, yet there are no questions that directly address this skill. The teacher has concerns with which aspect of the standardized test?

a. Validity
b. Reliability
c. Bias
d. Objectivity

38. In screening and assessment instruments, what is an example of test sensitivity?

a. How often a test over-identifies or under-identifies target problems
b. How much potential a test has to offend or harm the test-taker
c. How often a test accurately rules out a problem it is meant to test
d. How often a test accurately identifies a problem it is meant to test

39. Olivia receives her weekly paycheck and calculates that she will spend $\frac{1}{4}$ of it on groceries. If the groceries cost \$120, what is the amount of her paycheck?

a. \$360
b. \$425
c. \$480
d. \$600

40. Each base of a triangular prism has a base length of 7.5 cm and a height of 10 cm. The height of the prism is 12 cm. What is the volume of the prism?

a. 375 cm^3
b. 450 cm^3
c. 525 cm^3
d. 600 cm^3

41. A 6th grade math teacher is introducing the concept of positive and negative numbers to a group of students. Which of the following models would be the most effective when introducing this concept?

a. Fraction strips
b. Venn diagrams
c. Shaded regions
d. Number lines

42. A ball has a diameter of 7 inches. Which of the following best represents the volume?

a. 165.7 in^3
b. 179.6 in^3
c. 184.5 in^3
d. 192.3 in^3

43. The graph of the parent function $y = x^2$ is shifted 5 units to the left and 4 units down. Which of the following equations represents the transformed function?

a. $y = (x - 5)^2 - 4$
b. $y = (x + 5)^2 - 4$
c. $y = (x - 5)^2 + 4$
d. $y = (x + 5)^2 + 4$

44. Julia drops a ball from a second-story window. The height of the ball is modeled by the function $f(x) = -2.5x^2 + 2x + 9$, where $f(x)$ represents the height of the ball and x represents the number of seconds. Which of the following best represents the number of seconds that will pass before the ball reaches the ground?

a. 2.1
b. 2.3
c. 2.5
d. 2.8

45. What is the converse of the statement below?

If I see a robin, it is spring.

a. If it is not spring, I do not see a robin.
b. If it is spring, I do not see a robin.
c. If I do not see a robin, it is not spring.
d. If it is spring, I see a robin.

46. When given the equation $8B + 11 = 43$, a student found $B = 6.75$. What mistake did the student most likely make?

a. When isolating the like terms, the student divided incorrectly by 8.
b. When isolating like terms, the student added instead of subtracting 11 from the right side.
c. The student used the wrong order of operations.
d. The student forgot to isolate like terms.

47. A fourth-grade teacher is planning direct instruction for a unit on decimals and calculating simple percentages. Which of the following additional activities could this teacher implement to foster students' real-world connections to these concepts?

a. Creating a budget for a grocery shopping trip
b. Preparing and acting out a scene from a restaurant
c. Listing the ingredients from a favorite recipe
d. Solving word problems that include decimals and percentages

48. Kevin saves $3 during Month 1. During each subsequent month, he plans to save 4 more dollars than he saved during the previous month. Which of the following equations represents the amount he will save during the nth month?

a. $a_n = 3n - 1$
b. $a_n = 3n + 4$
c. $a_n = 4n + 3$
d. $a_n = 4n - 1$

49. Which of the following best represents the standard deviation of the data below?

3, 4, 4, 5, 6, 12, 12, 15

a. 2.9
b. 3.4
c. 4.1
d. 4.6

50. Which of the following statements is true?

a. The set of whole numbers is a subset of the set of natural numbers.
b. The set of integers is a subset of the set of natural numbers.
c. The set of integers is a subset of the set of rational numbers.
d. The set of rational numbers is a subset of the set of integers.

51. What is the constant of proportionality represented by the table below?

x	y
−3	9
0	0
2	−6
7	−21
12	−36

a. −12
b. −9
c. −3
d. 3

52. Which of the following characteristics accurately describes authentic assessment techniques?

a. They are norm-referenced
b. They are designed to build higher-order thinking skills
c. They allow students to choose from a set of teacher-prepared responses
d. They measure students' performance at a specific point in time

53. Mr. James wants his students to draw a square based on specific attributes he says aloud. Which of the following is the most precise definition he could give his students?

a. "This shape has 4 sides. The opposite sides are parallel to each other."
b. "This shape has 4 sides that are all the same length. The opposite sides are parallel to each other."
c. "This shape has 4 sides that are all the same length. Each side is at a 90° angle to the other sides it touches."
d. "This shape has 4 sides. Each side is at a 90° angle to the other sides it touches."

54. Which of the following formulas represents the sequence 8, 12, 16, 20, 24, ...?

a. $a_n = 8n + 4; n \in \mathbb{N}$
b. $a_n = 4n + 4; n \in \mathbb{N}$
c. $a_n = n + 8; n \in \mathbb{N}$
d. $a_n = 8n; n \in \mathbb{N}$

55. Which of the following graphs represents the solution to the system of inequalities below?

$$-2x + 3y \leq 3$$
$$-8x + 6y \geq -3$$

a.

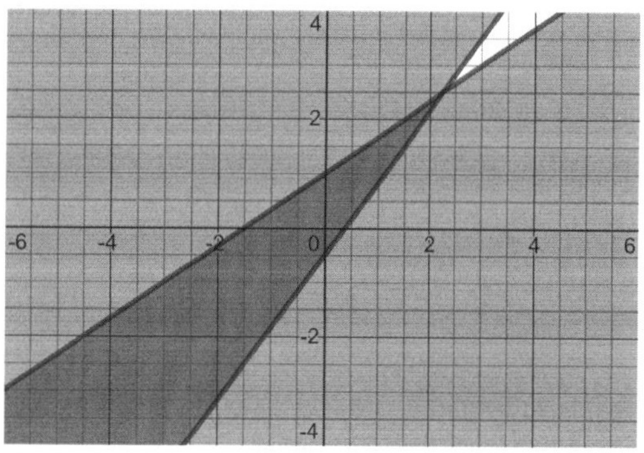

b.

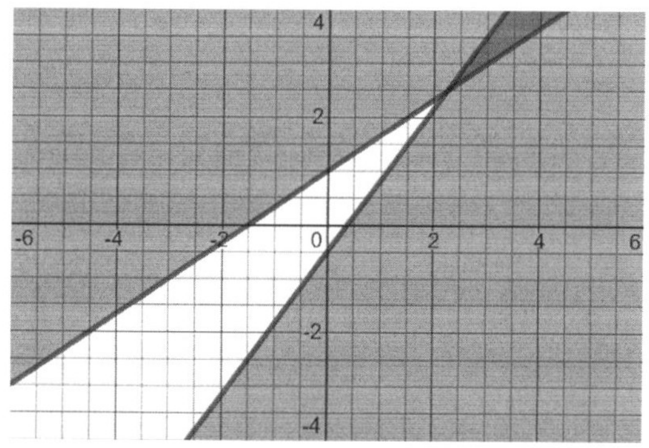

c.

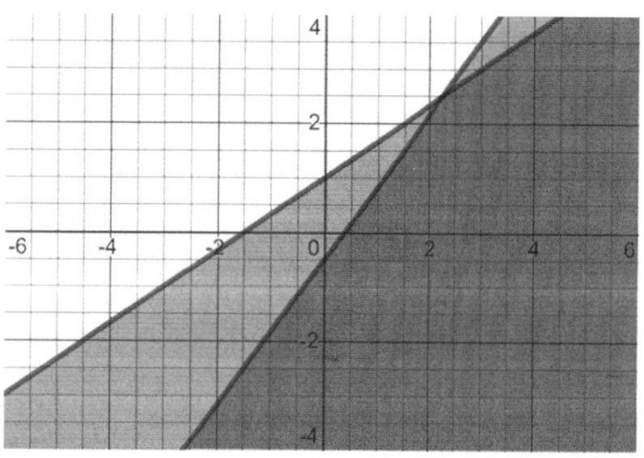

d.

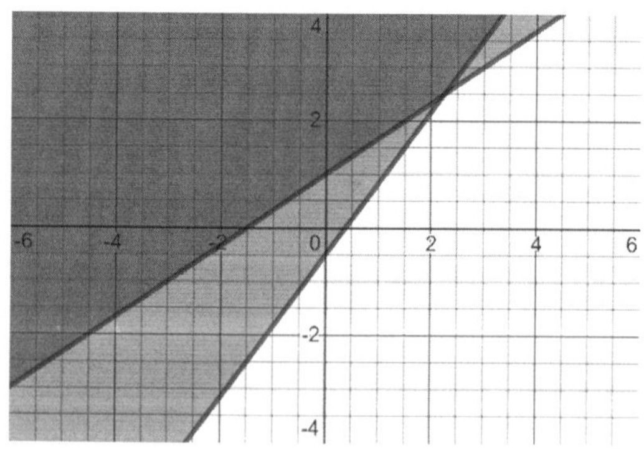

56. The values below represent a sample taken from a larger population. Which of the following best represents the standard deviation of the larger population?

$$\{8, 10, 11, 13, 13, 16, 17, 20\}$$

a. 2.9
b. 3.4
c. 4.0
d. 4.6

57. Sofia is learning to match equivalent fractions. Her homework question asks: "Circle the fraction(s) equivalent to $\frac{1}{2}$." The options given are: $\frac{2}{3}, \frac{2}{4}, \frac{3}{4}$, and $\frac{3}{6}$. Sofia circles $\frac{2}{3}$ and $\frac{3}{4}$. When her teacher asks her to explain her reasoning, what might Sofia say?

a. "I multiplied the top and the bottom of the fraction by the same numbers."
b. "I added the same numbers to the top and the bottom of the fraction."
c. "I drew a pie and split the $\frac{1}{2}$ into two pieces and into two more pieces."
d. "I drew three pies and split one into thirds, one into fourths, and one into sixths. Then I colored in the pies to match the fractions and circled the ones where I had colored in one half of the pie."

58. A city is at an elevation of 4,900 feet. Which of the following best represents the elevation in miles?

a. 0.93 miles
b. 0.98 miles
c. 1.08 miles
d. 1.21 miles

59. Which of the following describes a sampling technique that will likely increase the sampling error?

a. Alphabetizing names on a list and choosing every other name
b. Using a larger sample size
c. Replicating the study with new groups
d. Grouping a sample according to age and choosing the first 50 people

60. A 12-foot-tall tree casts a shadow that is 9.8 ft in length. Which of the following best represents the distance from the top of the tree to the end of the shadow?

a. 6.9 ft
b. 12.8 ft
c. 15.5 ft
d. 18.5 ft

61. Andrew rolls a die. What is the probability he gets a 4 or an even number?

a. $\frac{1}{4}$
b. $\frac{1}{2}$
c. $\frac{2}{3}$
d. $\frac{3}{4}$

62. A group of teachers are given a day to plan interdisciplinary units collaboratively prior to the beginning of a school year. What should these teachers do first to ensure that they plan effectively?

a. Create an outline of key concepts in each unit to see which concepts overlap between subjects.
b. Have each teacher discuss what they want to accomplish in the interdisciplinary unit.
c. Work together to create a detailed summative assessment for the unit that will assess each subject being taught.
d. Construct a list of what information they want students to learn from this unit.

63. Jeni buys a phone charger for $28. If it had been marked down 30%, what was the original cost?

a. $30
b. $32
c. $35
d. $40

64. The x-axis in the scatter plot below represents the number of miles Cyndi drives. The y-axis represents the gallons of gas left in her car's tank. About how many gallons will remain when she has driven 250 miles? Choose the best estimate.

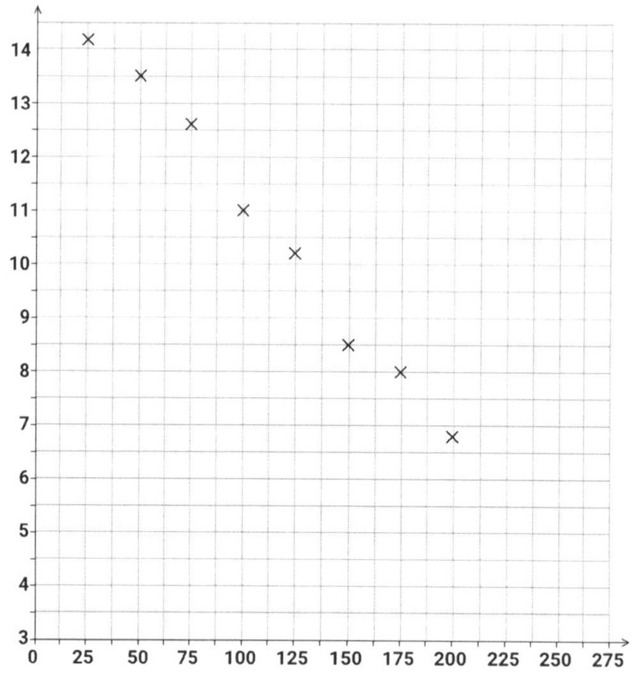

a. 3.5 gallons
b. 4.5 gallons
c. 5.5 gallons
d. 6.5 gallons

65. Given that the two horizontal lines in the diagram below are parallel, which of the following statements is correct?

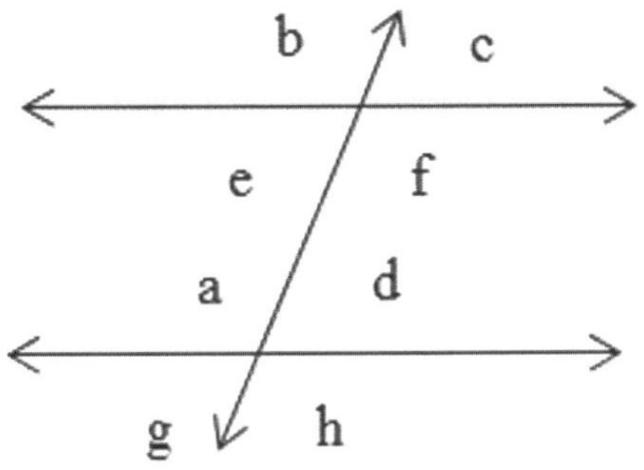

a. Angles b and g are complementary.
b. Angles d and c are supplementary.
c. Angles a and e are supplementary.
d. Angles e and h are congruent.

66. What is the length of the hypotenuse in the right triangle shown below?

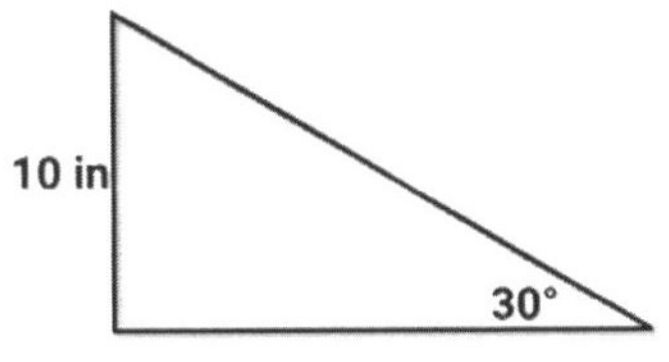

a. $\frac{20}{3}\sqrt{3}$ in
b. $10\sqrt{3}$ in
c. 20 in
d. $20\sqrt{3}$ in

67. Which of these is true about having an awareness of patterns and relationships in the real world?

a. It does not inform our understanding of the basic structure of things.
b. It helps us understand series of events, but not predict future ones.
c. It is unrelated to our basic feeling of confidence in the environment.
d. It increases our self-efficacy about interacting with our environment.

68. Which of the following pairs of equations represents the lines of symmetry in the figure below?

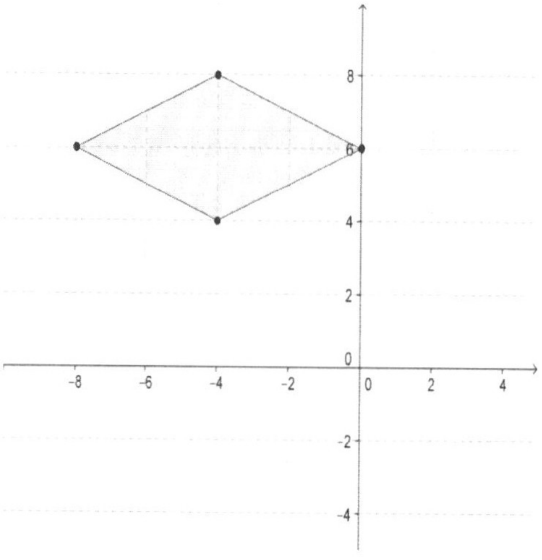

a. $x = -4, y = 6$
b. $x = 4, y = 6$
c. $y = -4, x = 6$
d. $y = 4, x = -6$

69. Which of these is/are most representative of using statistics in everyday life to predict probabilities?

a. An actuarial table in an insurance company
b. A weather forecast for the chances of rain
c. A chart comparing results of interventions
d. Answers (A) and (B) represent probability

70. Mark's nightstand currently holds 6 books, 12 pencils, and 1 highlighter. If he must place one item from each category into his backpack, how many possible selections are there?

a. 19
b. 72
c. 144
d. 180

71. Which of the following pairs of equations represents the lines of symmetry in the figure below?

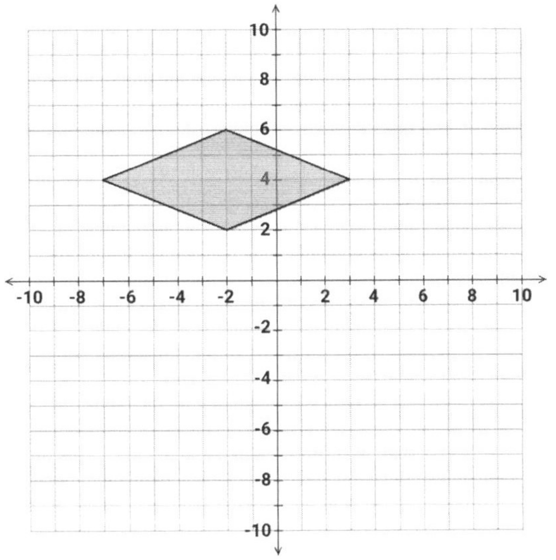

a. $x = -2, y = 4$
b. $x = 2, y = 4$
c. $y = -2, x = 4$
d. $y = 2, x = 4$

72. Ms. Byrne stresses the importance of daily math homework with her sixth- and seventh-grade students. She states that the consistent practice will help students solidify their understanding of mathematical principles. Ms. Byrne also reviews this homework on a daily basis to help her understand what the students understand and to guide her instruction. This practice is an example of:

a. Summative assessment
b. Diversity in assignments
c. Formative assessment
d. Standards set forth for middle-grade mathematics

73. Which of the following functions has a limit of 0?

a. $f(x) = 2x$
b. $f(x) = \frac{4}{x}$
c. $f(x) = \frac{x}{8}$
d. $f(x) = \frac{3x+1}{x}$

74. Which of the following is the best representation of 30,490 in scientific notation?

a. 3.049×10^{-4}
b. 3.049×10^{3}
c. 30.490×10^{3}
d. 3.049×10^{4}

75. For which of the following data sets would the mean be an appropriate measure of center to use?

a. 7, 7, 9, 10, 10, 11, 13, 14, 46, 50
b. 6, 8, 11, 15, 17, 17, 21, 22, 25, 25
c. 4, 9, 36, 41, 43, 44, 48, 48, 49, 50
d. 2, 91, 92, 96, 96, 98, 100, 102, 104, 105

76. What is the limit of the series below?

$$1 + \frac{2}{3} + \frac{4}{9} + \frac{8}{27} + \frac{16}{81} + \cdots$$

a. 2
b. $2\frac{1}{3}$
c. $2\frac{2}{3}$
d. 3

77. Mrs. Miller is teaching a unit on numbers and operations with her sixth-grade class. At the beginning of class, she asks the students to work in groups to sketch a Venn diagram to classify whole numbers, integers, and rational numbers on a white board. Which of the following types of assessments has the teacher used?

a. Summative assessment
b. Formative assessment
c. Formal assessment
d. Informal assessment

78. Adam rolls a standard six-sided die. What is the probability he rolls a number greater than or equal to 5?

a. $\frac{1}{6}$
b. $\frac{1}{5}$
c. $\frac{1}{4}$
d. $\frac{1}{3}$

79. What is the slope of the leg marked *x* in the triangle graphed below?

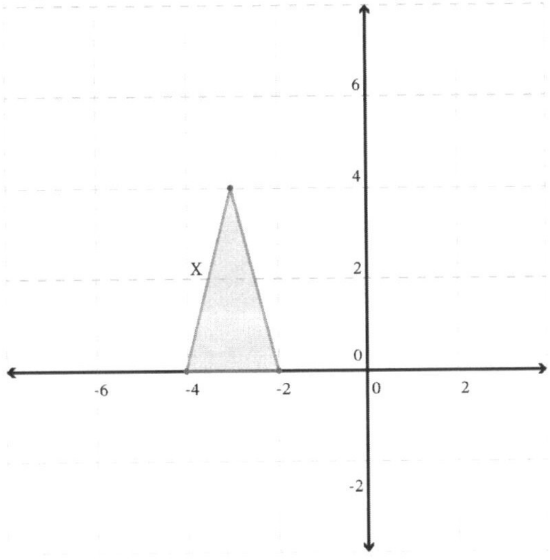

a. 2
b. 3.5
c. 4
d. 4.5

80. Laura buys 6 pens and 2 notebooks for $7.20. Julio buys 15 pens and 1 notebook for $12.60. How much does one notebook cost?

a. $0.50
b. $0.75
c. $1.35
d. $1.50

81. How many ways can you arrange the letters below, if order does NOT matter?

STATISTICS

a. 12,600
b. 25,200
c. 50,400
d. 100,800

Refer to the following for question 82:

The administrators at a middle school are considering implementing a team teaching model for sixth-grade classes in the upcoming school year. The administrators, including the principal and vice-principal, have convened a staff meeting to discuss this possibility with the sixth-grade teachers.

82. At the end of the year, the teachers decide that they want to evaluate the effectiveness of the team teaching model for their sixth-grade students. Which of the following research strategies would provide them with the best assessment of the model?

a. The teachers should compare this group of students' performance on standardized tests in previous years with their performance in sixth grade at the end of the year.
b. The teachers should compare the students' performance in classes that are part of the team teaching model (math, science, language arts, social studies) with their performance in classes that are not team-taught (health, physical education, art).
c. The teachers should compare their students' performance in sixth grade to the performance of sixth-grade students at schools that do not use team teaching.
d. The teachers should compare their sixth-grade students' performance this year with the performance of sixth-grade students in previous years where team teaching was not used; they should also consider the performance history of this particular group of sixth graders relative to previous groups.

83. You are asked to vote on the #1 and #2 performers from a list of 5 candidates. How many possible selections could you make?

a. 120
b. 100
c. 20
d. 10

84. When planning a unit on linear equations, a teacher would most likely include discussion on which of the following topics?

a. Conjugating to remove irrational denominators
b. Slope of a straight line
c. Order of operations
d. Characteristics of the diagonals of various quadrilaterals

85. The most effective way to structure a math session for the benefit of primary students is to:

a. Check all homework assignments and be sure that all workbook pages are completed
b. Focus almost entirely on computation skills
c. Focus almost entirely on the application of math skills to real-life situations
d. Divide class time evenly between computation skills and real-life applications

86. A car moves at a constant velocity. Which of the following accurately describes the appearance of the position-time graph?

a. It is a line with a positive slope.
b. It is a line with a negative slope.
c. It is a curve with an increasing slope.
d. It is a curve with a decreasing slope.

87. Which of the following represents an inversely proportional relationship?

a. $y = \frac{1}{x}$
b. $y = \frac{1}{2}x$
c. $y = x$
d. $y = x^2$

88. Danielle pays a fee of 0.1% of her paycheck for direct deposit into her bank account. If her monthly paycheck is $3,200, what will her fee be each month?

a. $0.32
b. $3.20
c. $32
d. $320

89. What is the approximate area of the shaded region between the circle and the square in the figure shown below? Use 3.14 for π.

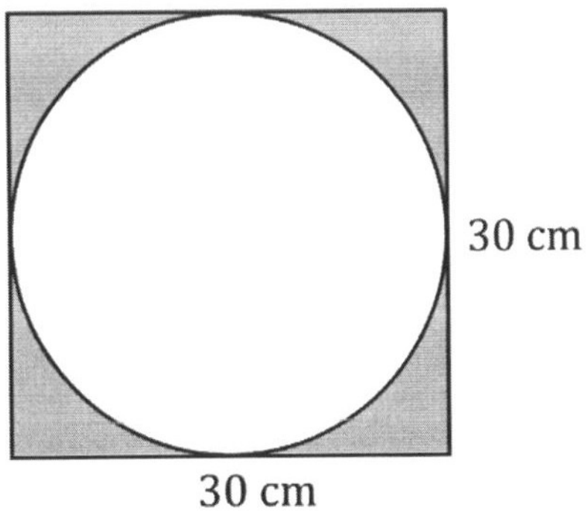

a. 177 cm²
b. 181 cm²
c. 187 cm²
d. 193 cm²

90. Meg buys a used car for $6,375. The original price had been marked down by 15%. What was the original price of the car?

a. $7,150
b. $7,375
c. $7,500
d. $7,775

91. By the end of what grade level should a student be able to use algebraic principles to analyze both proportional and non-proportional linear relationships?

a. 5th grade
b. 6th grade
c. 7th grade
d. 8th grade

92. What is $\lim_{n\to\infty} \frac{n^3-n^2}{n}$?

a. 0
b. 1
c. 2
d. There is no limit.

93. Maria uses the pie chart below to represent the allocation of her time on an average 24-hour school day.

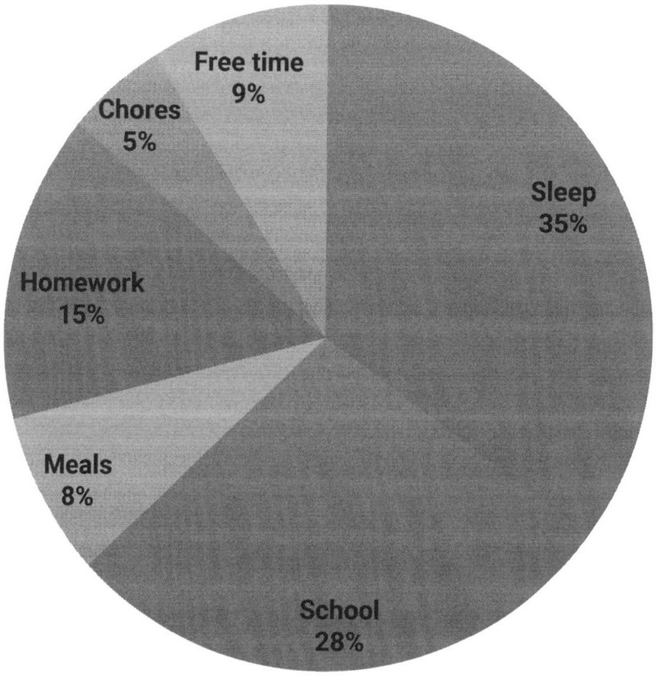

Which of the following statements is true?

a. The amount of time she spends on sleep is less than 8 hours per night.
b. The amount of time she spends on chores and free time is approximately 4 hours per day.
c. The amount of time she spends on meals and homework is more than 5 hours per day.
d. The amount of time she spends on school is more than 7 hours per day.

94. Andrea must administer $\frac{1}{12}$ of a medicine bottle to a patient. If the bottle contains $3\frac{4}{10}$ fluid ounces of medicine, how much medicine should be administered?

a. $\frac{17}{60}$ fluid ounces
b. $\frac{15}{62}$ fluid ounces
c. $\frac{3}{19}$ fluid ounces
d. $\frac{17}{67}$ fluid ounces

95. Given that the two horizontal lines in the diagram below are parallel, which of the following statements is correct?

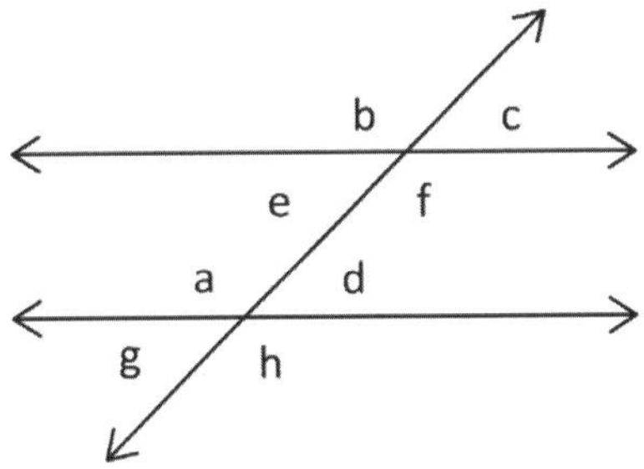

a. $\angle c$ and $\angle g$ are complementary.
b. $\angle c$ and $\angle h$ are supplementary.
c. $\angle a$ and $\angle f$ are supplementary.
d. $\angle g$ and $\angle h$ are congruent.

96. Kevin uses the pie chart below to represent how he spends his allowance. His monthly allowance is $50.

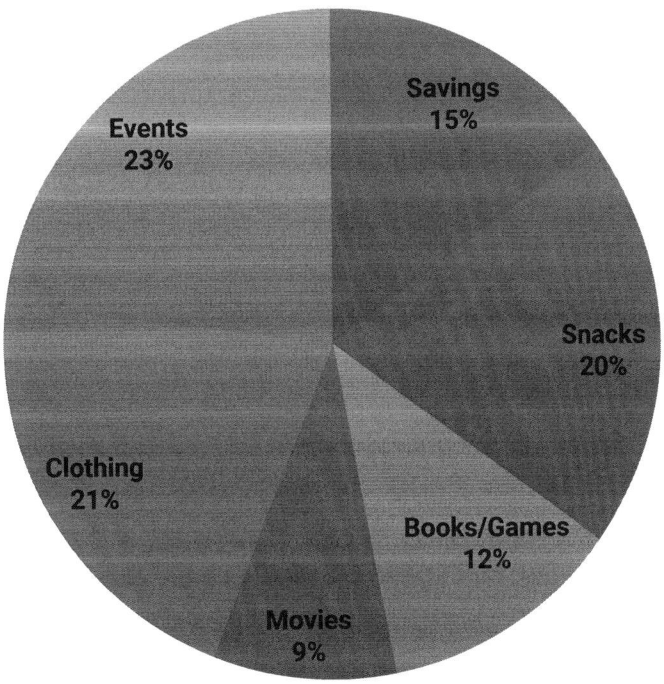

Which of the following statements is true?

a. The amount of money he spends on snacks is more than $10.
b. The amount of money he spends on movies, books, and games is more than $10.
c. The amount of money he spends on savings is less than $7.
d. The amount of money he spends on clothing and events is less than $10.

97. 75 students are surveyed. 36 of the students like only pepperoni pizza. 22 of the students like only supreme pizza. 12 of the students like neither kind of pizza. How many students like pepperoni *and* supreme pizza?

a. 2
b. 3
c. 4
d. 5

98. Dan rolls a standard six-sided die and tosses a coin. What is the probability he gets a non-prime number or tails?

a. $\frac{1}{2}$
b. $\frac{2}{3}$
c. $\frac{3}{4}$
d. $\frac{5}{6}$

99. Which of the following shapes is NOT a possible cross-section of a triangular prism?

a. Circle
b. Rectangle
c. Trapezoid
d. Triangle

100. Which of the following equations represents a line parallel to the one graphed below and passing through the point $(-1, 4)$?

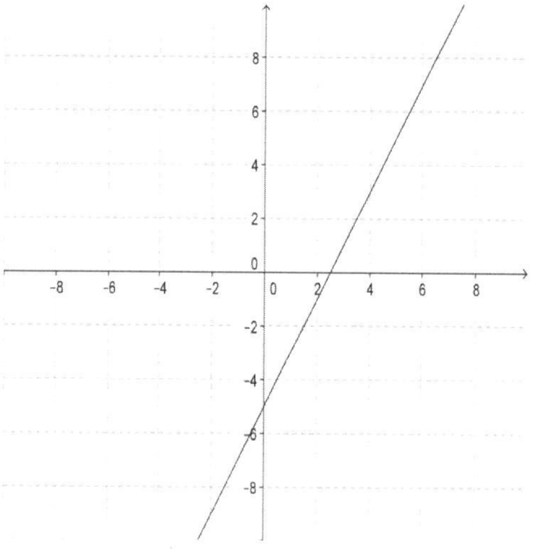

a. $y = 2x - 2$
b. $y = 3x + 6$
c. $y = 3x - 4$
d. $y = 2x + 6$

Constructed Response

1. Michael buys a new laptop for $1,850. The computer loses 10% of its value the day it is purchased and depreciates at a constant rate following that. The value of the computer as a function of time can be modeled by $y = c - 0.03cx$, where y is the value of the laptop x months after it was purchased and c is the value after the initial 10% depreciation.

Part A: What is the value of the laptop 1 year after its purchase date? Show your work.

Part B: On an xy-grid, graph the value, y, of the computer, as a function of x, where x represents the number of months after the purchase date, for $0 \leq x \leq 9$ months. Label the axes and show the scales used for the graph.

Part C: Use your graph to estimate the number of months, x, after the purchase date that the value of the laptop is $1,500. Label this point on your graph and indicate the approximate coordinates of the point.

Part D: Algebraically find the number of months, x, after the purchase date that the value of the laptop is exactly $1,500. Round your solution to the nearest tenth of a month. Show your work.

2. Gillian is planning a festival in her city square. The circular area below is the part of the square with available electricity and has been set aside for food vendors. There will be four square vendor spaces, each with a side of 10 feet, within the circular area (which has a diameter of 30 feet).

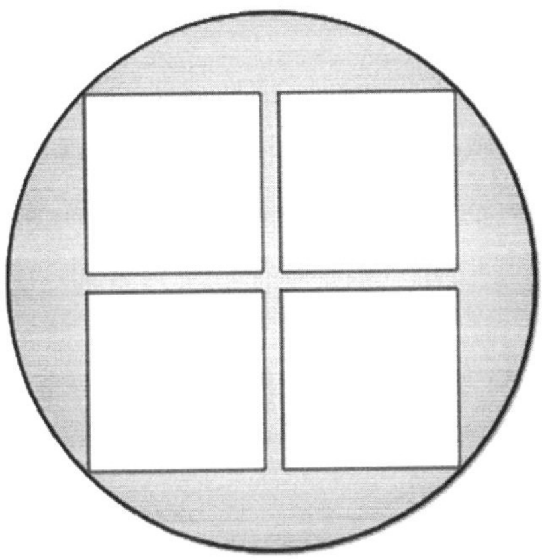

Part A: According to the diagram, what is the area, in square feet, that will be taken up by the vendors? Show your work.

Part B: According to the diagram, what percentage of the circle will be available for customers to walk among the vendors? Show your work.

Part C: If a random point is chosen within the circular area, what is the probability that it would fall in a vendor's booth? Show your work or explain your reasoning.

3. Below are listed the weights in pounds of the 16 students in a fourth-grade class.

51, 54, 54, 56, 59, 60, 62, 63, 64, 64, 67, 69, 69, 73, 76, 83

Part A: For the numbers above, define and identify the median and the range.

Part B: Define and calculate the mean for the list of numbers above.

Part C: Draw a stem and leaf plot of the data using the tens digits as the stems and the units digits as the leaves.

Answer Key and Explanations for Test #1

Multiple Choice

1. B: The net of a square pyramid has a square base and four triangular faces. So only choice B can be folded into a square pyramid. Choice A creates a triangular prism. Choice C does not create a proper 3D figure because the triangle sides overlap. Choice D creates a triangular pyramid.

2. D: The Pythagorean theorem may be used to find the diagonal distance from the top of his head to the base of the shadow. Using the following equation, we can determine this distance, c: $5.8^2 + 6.2^2 = c^2$. Thus, $c \approx 8.5$. The distance is approximately 8.5 ft.

3. C. The original price may be modeled by the equation:

$$(x - 0.45x) + 0.0875(x - 0.45x) = \$39.95$$

This simplifies to $0.598125x = \$39.95$. Dividing each side of the equation by the coefficient of x gives $x \approx \$66.79$.

4. C: The number in the sample space is equal to the number of possible outcomes for one coin toss, 2, raised to the power of the number of coin tosses, or 4. $2^4 = 16$.

5. A: The size of the sample space equals the number of possible outcomes for one coin toss, 2, raised to the power of the number of coin tosses, 3. So the sample space for tossing a coin three times is $2^3 = 8$.

6. C: Students should submit written samples of their work for the teacher to review on a daily basis. Standardized tests would not be appropriate for assessing the student's understanding of the given task. As students are likely to work on the problems at different times, classroom observation would not be practical, and group discussions would not necessarily be useful for assessment purposes.

7. B: Decreasing the sample size will likely increase the sampling error by increasing the likelihood of deviations from the true population. The other techniques utilize random sampling.

8. D: The slope of the graphed line is $\frac{1}{2}$. A line perpendicular to this one will have a slope of −2. Substituting the slope and the x- and y-values from the point $(1, -2)$ into the slope-intercept form of an equation gives: $-2 = -2(1) + b$, which simplifies to $-2 = -2 + b$. Adding 2 to each side of the equation gives $b = 0$; therefore, the equation of a line perpendicular to this one and passing through the point $(1, -2)$ is $y = -2x$.

9. C: The original price x may be modeled by the equation $(x - 0.35x) \times 1.0825 = 9.14$, which simplifies to $0.703625x = 9.14$. Dividing each side of the equation by the coefficient of x gives $x \approx 12.99$. The book was originally \$12.99.

10. A: A Venn diagram such as the one shown below may be drawn to assist in finding the answer.

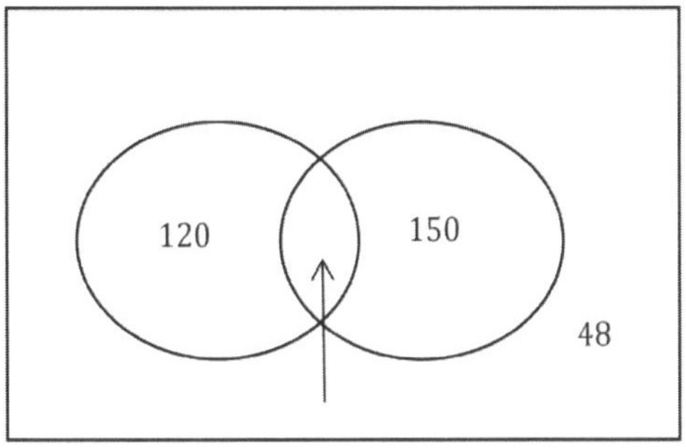

Since the set contains 320 total people, the solution is equal to $320 - (120 + 150 + 48)$ or 2 people.

11. B: The table shows the y-intercept to be 1. The slope is equal to the ratio of change in y-values to change in corresponding x-values. As each x-value increases by 1, each y-value decreases by 0.5. Thus, the slope is $\frac{-0.5}{1}$, or $-\frac{1}{2}$. This graph represents the equation $y = -\frac{1}{2}x + 1$.

12. C: In order for students to identify the relationship between counting and the concept of larger and smaller numbers, they must first understand that numbers represent objects and be able to accurately match the amount of objects to the corresponding number. However, this is not sufficient, as they must also understand the concept of larger and smaller. Some groups of objects have more items than other groups of objects. Once they can use numbers to represent amounts and determine which groups of objects are larger or smaller, then they can identify the relationship between these two concepts.

13. B: The distributive property of multiplication over addition is $a(b + c) = ab + ac$. Option B best prompts the usage of $2(5 + 8) = 2(5) + 2(8)$ by requiring students to find the total number of items by multiplying both the number of colored pencils and markers and adding them together. Choice A would test students' ability to apply order of operations to a word problem. Choice C asks students to answer two separate problems, which only require basic multiplication. Choice D would test students' ability to find the pertinent information in solving a word problem.

14. A: Kyra's monthly salary may be modeled as $\frac{1}{3}x = 1{,}050$. Multiplying both sides of the equation by 3 gives $x = 3{,}150$.

15. D: The constant of proportionality is equal to the slope. Using the points, (0,0) and (4,2), the slope may be written as $\frac{2-0}{4-0}$, which equals $\frac{1}{2}$.

16. C: The decimal expansion of an irrational number does not terminate or repeat. The number π is considered irrational because it does not terminate or repeat.

17. C: The product of $(x - 2)(5x + 7)$ equals $5x^2 + 7x - 10x - 14$, which simplifies to $5x^2 - 3x - 14$.

18. C: The strategy of planning which standards will be taught over the course of the school year and allocating the amount of time each topic will be taught is known as curriculum mapping. Backwards planning is when lessons are intentionally developed with a specific standard in mind. The assessment aligns closely to the standard being taught, and then the activities that would best support the standard are selected. Differentiation occurs when a teacher considers the needs of the students and incorporates choice into process, product, and content. Holistic assessment refers to evaluating a student globally through multiple data points.

19. D: The corresponding angles have congruent angle measures, each measuring 44°. According to the Corresponding Angles Converse Theorem, two lines are parallel if a transversal, intersecting the lines, forms congruent corresponding angles.

20. D: The constant of proportionality is equal to the slope. Using the points, $(2, -8)$ and $(5, -20)$, the slope may be written as $\frac{-20-(-8)}{5-2}$, which equals -4.

21. C: An inversely proportional relationship is written in the form $y = \frac{k}{x}$; thus, the equation $y = \frac{3}{x}$ shows that y is inversely proportional to x.

22. A: The value of the 35th term may be found using the formula $a_n = a_1 + (n-1)d$. Substituting the number of terms for n, the initial value of 1 for a, and the common difference of 2 for d gives: $a_{35} = 1 + (35-1)(2)$, which simplifies to $a_{35} = 69$. Now, the value of the 35th term may be substituted into the formula, $S_n = \frac{n(a_1+a_n)}{2}$, which gives: $S_{50} = \frac{35(1+69)}{2}$, which simplifies to $S_{35} = 1{,}225$.

23. D: The horizontal asymptote is equal to the ratio of the coefficient of $3x$ to the coefficient of $2x$, or $\frac{3}{2}$.

24. D: The following equation may be written and solved for x: $\sin 62° = \frac{x}{10}$. Multiplying both sides of the equation by 10 gives: $10 \times \sin 62° = x$, or $x \approx 8.8$.

25. C: Given the coefficients of the equations, the simplest procedure will be to use the elimination method, multiplying the first equation by two and summing them:

$$\begin{array}{r} 4x - 6y = 48 \\ \underline{5x + 6y = -21} \\ 9x + 0y = 27 \end{array}$$

Solve for x:

$$x = \frac{27}{9} = 3$$

Plug the value for x into one of the original equations:

$$2(3) - 3y = 24$$

$$3y = 6 - 24 = -18$$

$$y = -\frac{18}{3} = -6$$

Thus, the solution to the system of equations is $(3, -6)$.

26. A: Since the figures are similar, the following proportion may be written and solved for x: $\frac{8}{6} = \frac{6}{x}$. Thus, $x = \frac{36}{8}$ or $4\frac{1}{2}$.

27. D: If the statement is written in the form $p \rightarrow q$, then the contrapositive is represented as $\neg q \rightarrow \neg p$. Thus, the contrapositive should read, "If I do not go to the beach, then I do not get paid."

28. C: The set of irrational numbers is separate from the set of rational numbers. A rational number cannot be irrational, and an irrational number cannot be rational.

29. A: Given the coefficients of the equations, the simplest procedure will be to use the elimination method, multiplying the second equation by negative two and summing them:

$$\begin{array}{r} 4x - 2y = -38 \\ \underline{-4x - 6y = -34} \\ 0x - 8y = -72 \end{array}$$

Solve for y:

$$y = \frac{-72}{-8} = 9$$

Plug the value for y into one of the original equations:

$$4x - 2(9) = -38$$

$$4x - 18 = -38$$

$$4x = -20$$

$$x = -\frac{20}{4} = -5$$

Thus, the solution to the system of equations is $(-5,9)$.

30. B: The decimal expansion of an irrational number does not terminate or repeat. The decimal expansion of $\sqrt{2}$ does not terminate or repeat.

31. D: Since the pentagon is regular, all the sides are equal, and the shape is convex. Because of this, there are enough constraints to determine the area as a function of the side length of the pentagon.

32. D: The measure of the angle formed by the chord and the tangent is equal to one-half of the measure of the intercepted arc. Since the measure of the angle is 68°, the measure of the intercepted arc may be found by writing $68° = \frac{1}{2}x$. Dividing both sides of the equation by $\frac{1}{2}$ gives $x = 136°$. The measure of the intercepted arc may also be found by multiplying 68° by 2. Thus, the value of x is 136°.

33. B: At this level, it can often be difficult to sustain a productive discussion for longer than 15 minutes or so. After that, students will tend to lose interest or veer the discussion off topic.

34. C: Purchasing a DVD is a discretionary expense because it is based on personal desire rather than need. In other words, it is an expense made at the discretion of the consumer. Discretionary expenses are those over which a consumer has the most control. A comprehensive budget must include discretionary expenses as well as fixed and variable expenses. Fixed expenses, such as rent, are the same every month. Variable expenses, including groceries, school supplies, and heating oil, are always present but vary in amount over the course of a year.

35. C: Use of an intact group is called a convenience sample. Such a sample increases sampling error, since randomization was not employed. The other described techniques utilize random sampling.

36. C: The consecutive interior angles have supplementary angle measures, as 127° and 53° add up to 180°. According to the Consecutive Interior Angles Converse Theorem, two lines are parallel if a transversal, intersecting the lines, forms consecutive interior angles that are supplementary.

37. A: A test is valid if it measures what it is designed to measure. If a test claims to measure a student's ability to make inferences, then the questions on the test should require students to use this skill. Reliability refers to ensuring that there is consistency in test results over time and between participants. Bias refers to ensuring that the test does not put any participants at a disadvantage. Objectivity refers to ensuring that all tests are scored in the same manner without being affected by any outside influences or bias.

38. D: The definition of sensitivity in a test instrument is how often (typically measured in percentages) it accurately identifies a specific problem or disorder that it is designed to identify, e.g., a mental health disorder, a developmental delay, or a learning disability. If tests either over-identify or under-identify problems that are its targets (A), these are measurement errors rather than levels of sensitivity. Sensitivity in screening does not refer to adverse effects of a test on the person being tested (B), though this is a separate ethical concern if the test is harmful to the test cases. Sensitivity does not mean ruling out (C) a targeted condition. How often a test rules out a problem is often referred to as specificity.

39. C: Olivia's paycheck x may be modeled by $\frac{1}{4}x = 120$. Multiplying both sides of the equation by 4 gives $x = 480$. Her paycheck is \$480.

40. B: The volume of a prism may be calculated using the formula $V = Bh$, where B represents the area of the base and h represents the height of the prism. The area of each triangular base is represented by $A = \frac{1}{2}(7.5)(10)$. So, the area of each base is equal to 37.5 square centimeters. Substituting 37.5 for the area of the base and 12 for the height of the prism gives $V = (37.5)(12)$ or $V = 450$. The volume of the prism is 450 cm^3.

41. D: Number lines can help students understand the concepts of positive and negative numbers. Fraction strips are most commonly used with fractions. Venn diagrams are commonly used when comparing groups. Shaded regions are commonly used with fractions or percentages.

42. B: The volume of a sphere may be calculated using the formula $V = \frac{4}{3}\pi r^3$, where r represents the radius. Substituting 3.5 for r gives $V = \frac{4}{3}\pi(3.5)^3$, which simplifies to $V \approx 179.6 \text{ in}^3$.

43. B: Inside the squared term, the sign of the constant is positive for a shift to the left and negative for a shift to the right. Thus, a movement of 5 units left is indicated by $y = (x + 5)^2$. A shift of 4 units down is indicated by subtracting 4 units from the squared term, giving $y = (x + 5)^2 - 4$.

44. B: A graph of the function shows the positive x-intercept to occur at approximately (2.3,0). Thus, the ball will reach the ground after approximately 2.3 seconds.

45. D: If the statement is written in the form $p \rightarrow q$, then the converse is represented as $q \rightarrow p$. Thus, the converse should read, "If it is spring, I see a robin."

46. B: When learning to solve algebraic equations, it is necessary to treat the two sides of an equation equally. In order to isolate the variable, the first step is to subtract the constant from both sides. In this case, the constant is 11. By reworking the problem using the suggestion found in choice B, it is possible to arrive at the student's incorrect answer. The best method to solving this question is to use a trial and error method, determining which answer yields the incorrect answer.

47. B: As many mathematical concepts are abstract in nature, implementing concrete learning opportunities is beneficial in providing students with a real-world context to strengthen understanding. Doing so demonstrates the applications of math in everyday life, thus helping students build personal connections to learning that make the overall experience more relevant and meaningful. An assignment in which students prepare and act out a skit from a restaurant requires them to apply knowledge of decimals when selecting items from the menu and calculating their bill and use percentages when determining the tax and tip. Such an activity illustrates the real-world applications of these concepts by placing them in a familiar setting. Further, incorporating dramatic play into math instruction allows young students to process, organize, and ultimately internalize new information for greater retention.

48. D: This situation may be modeled by an arithmetic sequence, with a common difference of 4 and an initial value of 3. Substituting the common difference and initial value into the formula, $a_n = a_1 + (n-1)d$, gives $a_n = 3 + (n-1)(4)$, which simplifies to $a_n = 4n - 1$.

49. D: The standard deviation is equal to the square root of the ratio of the sum of the squares of the deviation of each score from the mean to the square root of the difference of n and 1. The mean of the data set is 7.625. The deviations are −4.625, −3.625, −3.625, −2.625, −1.625, 4.375, 4.375, and 7.375. The sum of the squares of the deviations may be written as:

$$21.39 + 13.14 + 13.14 + 6.89 + 2.64 + 19.14 + 19.14 + 54.39 = 149.87$$

Division of this sum by $n - 1 = 7$ gives 21.41. The square root of this quotient is approximately 4.6.

50. C: The set of integers is contained within the set of rational numbers and is therefore a subset of the rational numbers. A rational number may be written as the ratio, $\frac{a}{b}$, where a and b are integers and $b \neq 0$.

51. C: The constant of proportionality is equal to the slope. Using the points $(-3,9)$ and $(0,0)$, the slope may be written as $\frac{0-9}{0-(-3)}$, which equals −3.

52. B: Authentic assessment techniques are designed to build higher-order thinking skills because they require students to construct their own answers instead of choosing from preselected answers. They also allow for the possibility that multiple "correct" answers are possible because students bring different perspectives and prior experiences to the material. They typically measure student performance over an extended period of time and are graded on a criterion-referenced basis (e.g., students are compared to an objective standard, rather than being directly compared to one another).

53. C: Choice A could be any parallelogram. Choice B could be any rhombus, and choice D could be any rectangle. Choice C best matches the mathematical definition of a square (a plane figure with four equal sides and four right (90°) angles).

54. B: The sum of 4 and the product of each term number and 4 equals the term value. For example, for term number 3, the value is equal to $4(3) + 4$, or 16.

55. A: The test point of (0,0) indicates that shading should occur above the line with the steeper slope. The same test point indicates that shading should occur below the other line. The overlapped shading occurs between these two lines, in the lower left.

56. C: For a data sample with n values x_1 to x_n, with mean value $\bar{x}$, the formula for standard deviation is:

$$s = \sqrt{\frac{\sum_{i=1}^{n}(x_i - \bar{x})^2}{n-1}}$$

The mean of this data sample is $\bar{x} = 13.5$. The values for $(x_i - 13.5)$ are −5.5, −3.5, −2.5, −0.5, −0.5, 2.5, 3.5, and 6.5. The sum of the squares of these terms is:

$$\sum_{k=1}^{8}(x_k - 13.5)^2 = 30.25 + 12.25 + 6.25 + 0.25 + 0.25 + 6.25 + 12.25 + 42.25 = 110$$

Substituting this value into the original formula, we get:

$$s = \sqrt{\frac{110}{8-1}} \approx 4.0$$

57. B: If Sofia had correctly used the techniques described in choice A or choice D, she would have arrived at the correct answers, $\frac{2}{4}$ and $\frac{3}{6}$. Choice C would have shown her that $\frac{2}{4}$ and $\frac{4}{8}$ are equivalent fractions of $\frac{1}{2}$. By adding equal numbers to the numerator and denominator of $\frac{1}{2}$, Sophia concluded that $\frac{2}{3}$ and $\frac{3}{4}$ were equivalent fractions.

58. A: The following proportion may be written and solved for x: $\frac{5{,}280}{1} = \frac{4{,}900}{x}$. Thus, $x \approx 0.93$.

59. D: Choosing either the 50 youngest or 50 oldest people in a group is likely to increase sampling error, since randomization was not employed. The other described techniques utilize random sampling or other methods of decreasing sampling error.

60. C: The Pythagorean theorem may be used to find the diagonal distance from the top of the tree to the base of the shadow. Using the following equation, we can determine this distance, c: $12^2 + 9.8^2 = c^2$. Thus, $c \approx 15.5$. The distance is approximately 15.5 ft.

61. B: Since they are not mutually exclusive events, $P(4 \text{ or } E) = P(4) + P(E) - P(4 \text{ and } E)$. Substituting the probability of each event gives $P(4 \text{ or } E) = \frac{1}{6} + \frac{1}{2} - \frac{1}{6} = \frac{1}{2}$.

62. A: Creating an outline of key concepts to see which ones overlap between subjects is the first step teachers should take when planning interdisciplinary units. This will allow the teachers to see which skills overlap that they can target in instruction. While teachers should be able to discuss what they want to individually accomplish in the unit, this should not be the first step. Creating a summative assessment should be one of the first steps for planning the unit, but they should first identify which concepts they want students to learn before planning the assessment. Likewise, constructing a list of what information they want students to learn is helpful, but this needs to happen after outlining the key concepts from each subject in the interdisciplinary unit.

63. D: The original cost may be represented by the equation $28 = x - 0.3x$ or $28 = 0.7x$. Dividing both sides of the equation by 0.7 gives $x = 40$.

64. B: The points may be entered into a graphing calculator to find the least-squares regression line. This line is approximately $y = -0.044x + 15.59$. Substituting 250 for x gives $y = -0.044(250) + 15.59 = 4.59$. Thus, 4.5 gallons is a good estimate for the amount of gas that will be left after 250 miles.

Alternatively, if you visually predict a line of best fit using any two points, for example, the points (25,14.2) and (100,11), the slope between those points is approximately -0.043, and the line passes through the y-axis around $y = 15$. Using slope-intercept form ($y = mx + b$, where m is the slope and b is the y-intercept), we get the equation $y = -0.043x + 15$. At $x = 250$ we get $y = -0.043(250) + 15 = 4.25$. Thus, another good estimate would be 4.25 gallons, which is also close to 4.5.

65. C: When two parallel lines are cut by a transversal, the consecutive angles formed inside the lines are supplementary.

66. C: The triangle is a 30-60-90 right triangle. Thus, if the short leg is represented by x, the hypotenuse is represented by $2x$, and the long leg is represented by $x\sqrt{3}$. Thus, the hypotenuse is equal to 20 inches.

67. D: Being aware that patterns (regular repetitions) and relationships (associations between/among things) exist in the world affords us greater self-efficacy about our interacting with the environment, as well as increases our sense of confidence in the environment itself (C). This awareness not only helps us to understand sequences of events; it moreover enables us to predict the next event in the series before it occurs (B). Having an awareness of patterns and relationships in things also informs our understanding of the basic structure of those things (A).

68. A: The vertical line of symmetry is represented by an equation of the form $x = a$. The horizontal line of symmetry is represented by an equation of the form $y = b$. One line of symmetry occurs at $x = -4$. The other line of symmetry occurs at $y = 6$.

69. D: Both an insurance company's actuarial table (A) and a weather forecast for the chances of rain (B) predict the probability or likelihood of something happening—for an individual's illness, injury, or death by a given age (A), or for precipitation to occur in a given day or week (B). A chart comparing the results of different interventions (C) organizes and allows people to interpret data related to which method was more or less effective with certain populations rather than predicting the likelihood of any occurrence.

70. B: This is a counting problem. The number of possible selections equals the product of the possibilities for each category: $6 \times 12 \times 1 = 72$. There are 72 ways for Mark to fill his backpack.

71. A: The vertical line of symmetry is represented by an equation of the form $x = a$. The horizontal line of symmetry is represented by an equation of the form $y = a$. One line of symmetry occurs at $x = -2$. The other line of symmetry occurs at $y = 4$.

72. C: Formative assessment refers to any kind of evaluation by a teacher that helps guide her instruction. In mathematics instruction, teachers need to know exactly what the students have mastered in order to teach them appropriately because so many principles must be taught consecutively and in appropriate order. Conversations, class work and homework are all examples of formative assessments. These practices help teachers know where students might need more help and where instruction should be focused.

73. B: As the denominator approaches infinity, the value of the function will get smaller and smaller and converge to 0.

74. D: In scientific notation, only one digit should remain to the left of the decimal. In the original number, the decimal point is four places to the right of the first digit, 3. Therefore, $30{,}490 = 3.049 \times 10^4$ is the correct answer. Choice C, 30.490×10^3 is equal to the correct value, but it incorrectly places two digits to the left of the decimal point.

75. B: Data sets A and C are asymmetrical. Data set A is skewed toward lower values, and data set C is skewed toward higher values. This makes the mean a poor measure of center. Data set D is mostly symmetrical but has a small outlier. The mean is very sensitive to outliers and is not an appropriate measure of center for data sets that include them. Data set B is roughly symmetrical and has no outliers. The mean would be an appropriate measure of center here.

76. D: The series is an infinite geometric series. The sum may be calculated using the formula $S = \frac{a}{1-r}$, where a represents the value of the first term and r represents the common ratio. Substituting 1 for a and $\frac{2}{3}$ for r gives $S = \frac{1}{1-\frac{2}{3}}$ or 3.

77. B: This is a formative assessment because she is assessing students while she is still teaching the unit. Summative assessments are given at the end of the unit. Formal assessments are usually quizzes or tests. Informal assessments include asking individual students questions. Therefore, the correct choice is (B).

78. D: The number of outcomes in the event is 2 (rolling a 5 or 6), and the sample space is 6 (numbers 1 to 6). Thus, the probability may be written as $\frac{2}{6}$, which simplifies to $\frac{1}{3}$.

79. C: The slope may be written as $m = \frac{4-0}{-3-(-4)}$, which simplifies to $m = 4$.

80. C: The situation may be modeled by the system $\begin{cases} 6x + 2y = 7.20 \\ 15x + y = 12.60 \end{cases}$. One way to solve this system is to multiply the bottom equation by −2.

$$\begin{cases} 6x + 2y = 7.20 \\ -30x - 2y = -25.20 \end{cases}$$

Then, add the two equations and solve for x.

$$-24x = -18$$
$$x = 0.75$$

Thus, one pen costs $0.75. We can plug this value back into the second equation and solve for y to find the price of one notebook.

$$15(0.75) + y = 12.60$$
$$11.25 + y = 12.60$$
$$y = 1.35$$

Therefore, one notebook costs $1.35.

81. C: The number of ways the letters can be arranged may be represented as $\frac{10!}{3!3!2!1!1!}$, which equals 50,400.

82. D: In order to assess the effectiveness of the team teaching model, the teachers should compare their sixth-grade students' performance this year with the performance of sixth-grade students in previous years where team teaching was not used. This will eliminate the possibility of differences among schools that would be present if they compared their students to students in other schools (C). Comparing their performance on standardized testing to the previous year (A) would not be a good measure of the success of the team teaching model, as students are expected to progress between grades. Comparing their performance in team teaching classes to their performance in other classes (B) also would not be a good assessment, as these classes require different skills and test different areas.

83. C: This situation describes a permutation, since order matters. The number of permutations of length r from a set of n elements is $P(n,r) = \frac{n!}{(n-r)!}$. This situation may be represented as $P(5,2) = \frac{5!}{(5-2)!} = \frac{5\times4\times3!}{3!} = 5 \times 4 = 20$. Therefore, there are 20 ways to rank the top 2 performers from a group of 5 candidates.

84. B: The slope of a straight line is a vital concept to understanding linear equations.

85. D: Students need to learn and practice computation skills, but they also need to learn that the mathematical skills they acquire in the classroom have practical value in their lives outside of school.

86. A: The position of the car is changing according to a constant speed. Thus, the graph will show a straight line with a positive but constant slope.

87. A: An inversely proportional relationship is written in the form $y = \frac{k}{x}$, thus the equation $y = \frac{1}{x}$ shows that y is inversely proportional to x.

88. B: The amount she pays is equal to 0.001(3,200). Thus, she pays $3.20.

89. D: The area of the square is $A = s^2 = (30 \text{ cm})^2 = 900 \text{ cm}^2$. The area of the circle is $A = \pi r^2 = (3.14)(15 \text{ cm})^2 \approx 707 \text{ cm}^2$. The area of the shaded region is equal to the difference between the area of the square and the area of the circle, or $900 \text{ cm}^2 - 707 \text{ cm}^2$, which equals 193 cm^2.

90. C: The original price may be represented by the equation $6{,}375 = x - 0.15x$ or $6{,}375 = 0.85x$. Dividing both sides of the equation by 0.85 gives $x = 7{,}500$.

91. D: Students in 8th grade should be able to use basic algebraic concepts to analyze both proportional and non-proportional linear relationships. Remember that in a proportional relationship between x and y, the ratio between the two variables is constant. In a non-proportional relationship, the ratio is varied; in other words, the graph of the ratio between x and y will not be a straight line. Algebraic concepts are introduced in previous grades, but this standard is not expected to be used consistently until 8th grade.

92. D: We first factor the numerator: $n^2(n-1)$. We can then write the expression as $\frac{n^2(n-1)}{n}$, which reduces to $n(n-1)$. As the limit approaches infinity, both n and $n-1$ increase without bound, so the expression has no limit.

93. C: The amount of time she spends on meals and homework is equal to $0.23(24)$, or 5.52, which is more than 5.

94. A: The amount to be administered may be written as $\frac{1}{12} \times \frac{34}{10}$, which equals $\frac{17}{60}$. Thus, she should administer $\frac{17}{60}$ fluid ounces of medicine.

95. B: When two parallel lines are cut by a transversal, the consecutive angles formed inside the lines are supplementary.

96. B: The amount he spends on movies, books, and games is equal to $0.21(50)$, or $\$10.50$, which is more than $\$10$.

97. D: A Venn diagram may be drawn to assist in finding the answer.

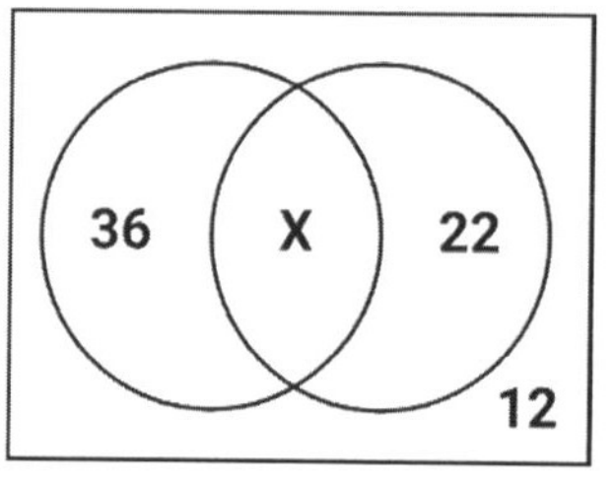

Since the set contains 75 total people, the solution is equal to $75 - (36 + 22 + 12)$ or 5 people.

98. C: Since they are not mutually exclusive events, the probability may be written as $P(N \text{ or } T) = P(N) + P(T) - P(N \text{ and } T)$. Because the events are independent, $P(N \text{ and } T) = P(N) \times P(T)$. Substituting the probability of each event gives $(N \text{ or } T) = \frac{1}{2} + \frac{1}{2} - \left(\frac{1}{2} \times \frac{1}{2}\right)$, or $\frac{3}{4}$.

99. A: The cross-section of a triangular prism will never be a circle. The cross-section of a polyhedron, such as a triangular prism, is always a polygon.

100. D: The slope of the graphed line is 2. A line parallel to this one will also have a slope of 2. Substituting the slope and the x- and y-values from the point $(-1,4)$ into the slope-intercept form of an equation gives $4 = 2(-1) + b$, which simplifies to $4 = -2 + b$. Adding 2 to both sides of the equation gives $b = 6$. So, the equation of a line parallel to this one and passing through the point $(-1,4)$ is $y = 2x + 6$.

Constructed Response

1. Part A: First, according to the problem, c is the value of the computer after its initial depreciation. The laptop's value drops by 10%, so:

$$c = \$1{,}850 - (0.1) \times (\$1{,}850) = \$1{,}665$$

Using this value for c and substituting it in, the value formula then becomes:

$$y = \$1{,}665 - (0.03) \times (\$1{,}665) \times (x)$$

Finally, since 1 year is 12 months, solve for y when $x = 12$:

$$y = \$1{,}665 - (0.03) \times (\$1{,}665) \times (12)$$
$$y = \$1{,}665 - \$599.40$$
$$y = \$1{,}065.60$$

Part B: The graph of y will be linear since x is raised to the first power. Reordering the function to the $y = mx + b$ format, the y-intercept and slope are readily identifiable:

$$y = \$1{,}665 - \left(\frac{\$49.95}{month}\right) \times (x)$$
$$y = -\left(\frac{\$49.95}{month}\right) \times (x) + \$1{,}665$$

Thus, the slope is $-\$49.95$ per month and the y-intercept is $\$1{,}665$. Plotting this function looks like the following.

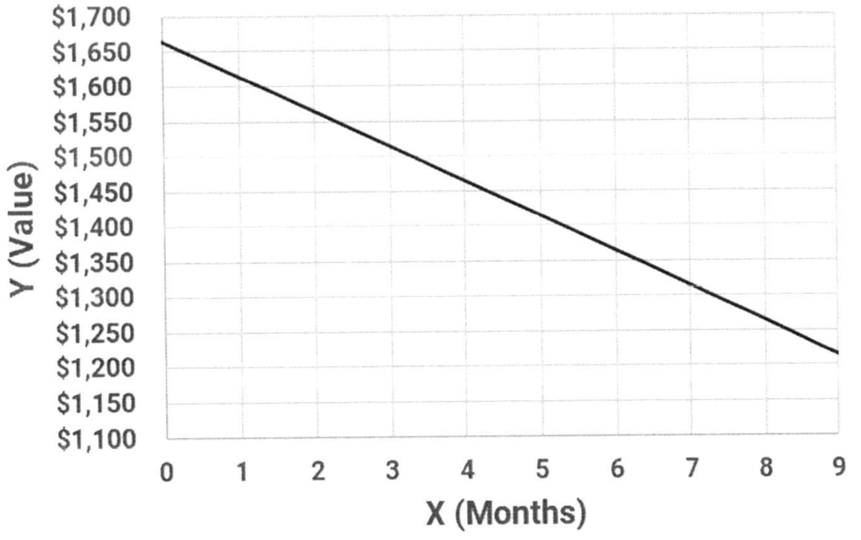

Part C: Using the axis values, it is readily apparent that the value function approaches $1,500 a little after 3 months. We can estimate that it is about 3.5 months from the graph.

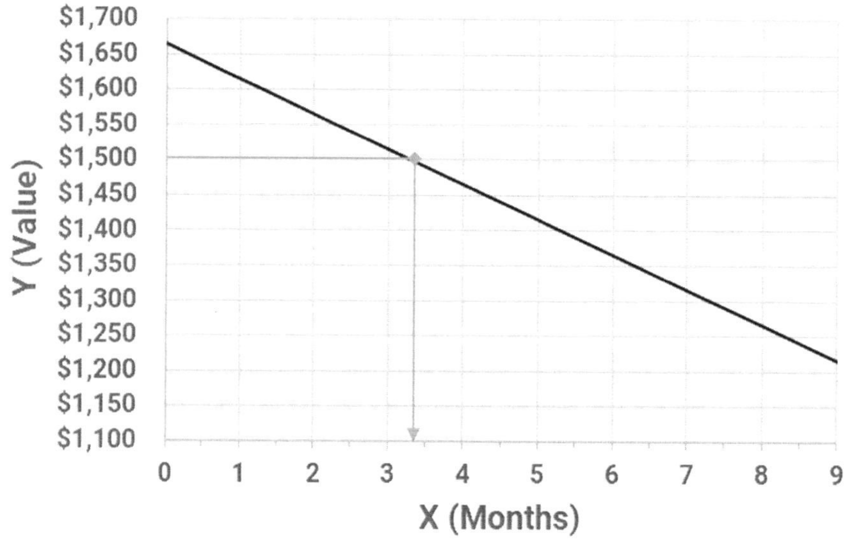

Part D: The way to use the function to find when the value is $1,500 is to substitute it in for y and solve for x:

$$\$1{,}500 = \$1{,}665 - \left(\frac{\$49.95}{month}\right) \times (x)$$
$$-\$165 = -\left(\frac{\$49.95}{month}\right) \times (x)$$
$$\frac{-\$165}{-\left(\frac{\$49.95}{month}\right)} = x$$
$$x = 3.303 \text{ months}$$

After rounding to the tenths place: $x = 3.3$ months

2. Part A: The vendor area is in the 4 squares only. We can find the area of one square and multiply by 4 to get the total vendor area. Since each side is 10 ft:

$$A_{vendors} = 4 \times s^2$$
$$A_{vendors} = 4 \times (10 \text{ ft})^2$$
$$A_{vendors} = 400 \text{ ft}^2$$

Part B: The first step in finding the percent walkway area is to find the area of the circle, which can be written as πr^2. Since the diameter is 30 ft, we know that the radius is 15 ft:

$$A = \pi \times (15 \text{ ft})^2$$
$$A \cong 706.5 \text{ ft}^2$$

Next, we can use the information from part A to find the area of the circle minus the area of the vendor booths to give us the total walking area. If the total area of the circle is approximately 706.5 ft^2 and the area of the vendor booths is 400 ft^2, then the area within the circle but around the booths is $706.5 - 400 \cong 306.5\ \text{ft}^2$.

The percent walkway area is found by:

$$walkway\% = \frac{A_{walkway}}{A_{circle}} \times 100\%$$

$$walkway\% \cong \frac{306.5\ \text{ft}^2}{706.5\ \text{ft}^2} \times 100\%$$

$$walkway\% \cong 43.4\%$$

Part C: It can be assumed that a point has an equal chance of being anywhere in the area of the circle. Thus, the probability it will land in a vendor area is given by:

$$P_{vendor} = \frac{A_{vendor}}{A_{circle}} \cong \frac{400\ \text{ft}^2}{706.5\ \text{ft}^2} \cong 0.566$$

3. Part A: The median of a list of values is the centermost value of an ordered list. If the ordered list has an even number of members, then the median is the average of the two centermost values. The two center values in this list are 63 and 64, so we add them and divide by 2 to find the median. The range of a list is the difference of the highest value and the lowest value. Thus, for this problem, the median is $\frac{63+64}{2} = 63.5$ lb and the range is $83 - 51 = 32$ lb.

Part B: The mean of a list of values is the sum of all the members of the list divided by the number of members in the list:

$$\text{mean} = \frac{51 + 2(54) + 56 + 59 + 60 + 62 + 63 + 2(64) + 67 + 2(69) + 73 + 76 + 83}{16}$$

$$\text{mean} = 64\ \text{lb}$$

Part C: The stem and leaf plot would look like this:

Stem	Leaves
5	1 4 4 6 9
6	0 2 3 4 4 7 9 9
7	3 6
8	3

Practice Test #2

Multiple Choice

1. Myles has a $60 budget to purchase a team lunch. He plans to buy sandwiches and salads. He needs to purchase a minimum of 15 items to make sure everyone has food. Each sandwich costs $3 and each salad costs $5. Which of the following graphs correctly shows the possible combinations of sandwiches and salads that he may buy, assuming that the x-axis represents sandwiches and the y-axis represents salads?

a.

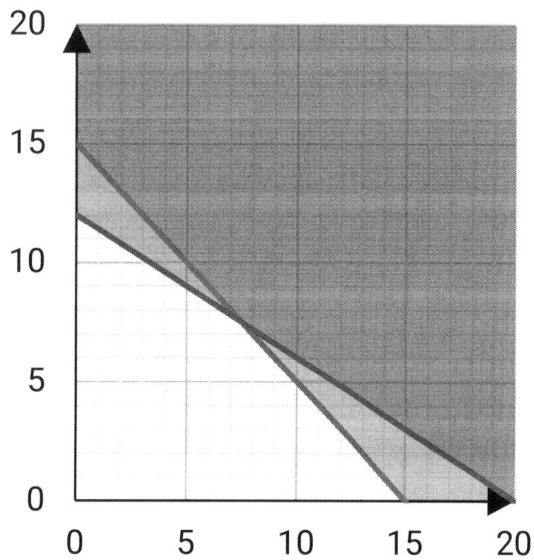

b.

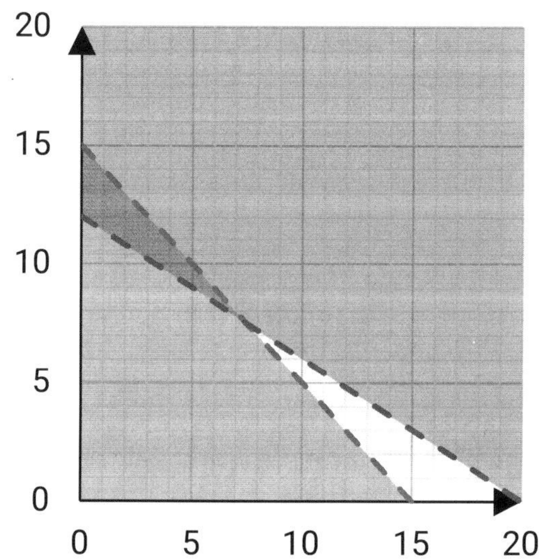

c.

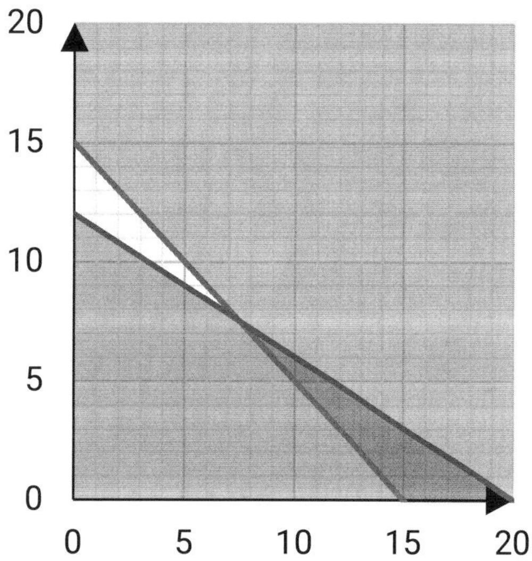

d.

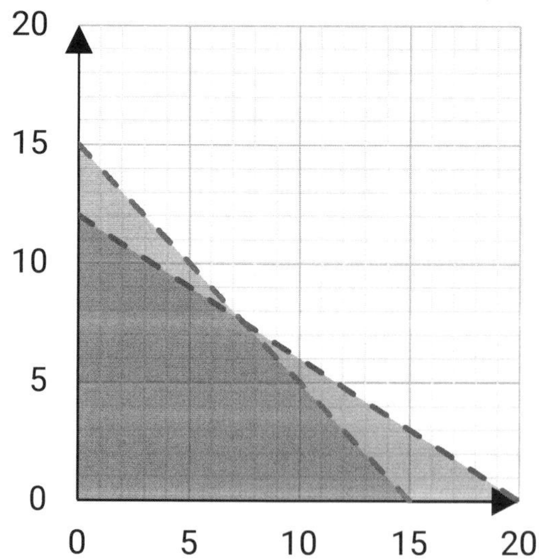

2. Mrs. Vories, a fifth-grade teacher, asks her class to use compatible numbers to help her determine approximately how many chicken nuggets she needs to buy for a school-wide party. The school has 589 students and each student will be served nine nuggets. Which student correctly applied the concept of compatible numbers?

a. Madison estimates: $500 \times 10 = 5{,}000$ nuggets
b. Audrey estimates: $600 \times 5 = 3{,}000$ nuggets
c. Ian estimates: $600 \times 10 = 6{,}000$ nuggets
d. Andrew estimates: $500 \times 5 = 2{,}500$ nuggets

3. What is the length of the hypotenuse in the right triangle shown below?

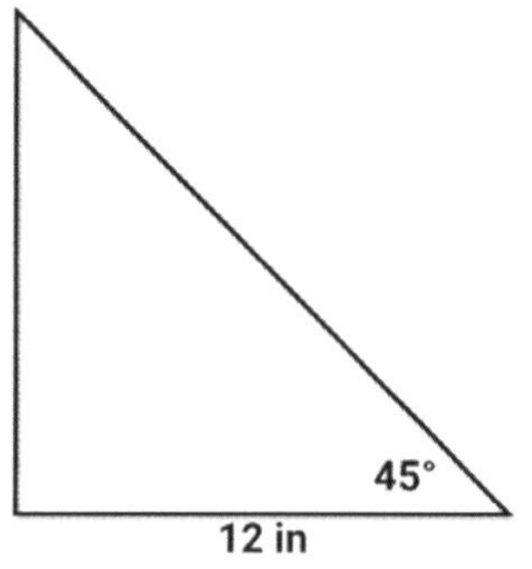

a. 15 in
b. $12\sqrt{3}$ in
c. 18 in
d. $12\sqrt{2}$ in

4. What is the midpoint of the line segment below?

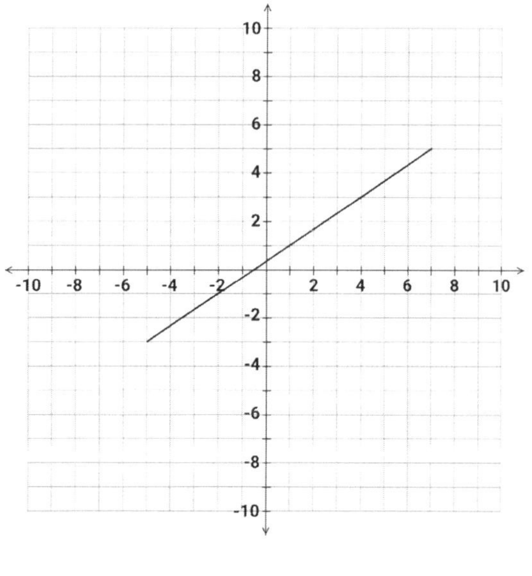

a. $(-0.5,2)$
b. $(1,1)$
c. $(1.5,3)$
d. $(2,1.5)$

5. A building is 44 feet tall and casts a shadow that is 59.2 ft in length. Which of the following best represents the distance from the top of the building to the end of the shadow?

a. 39.6 ft
b. 45.5 ft
c. 61.9 ft
d. 73.8 ft

6. Which of the following postulates may be used to prove the similarity of ΔABC and ΔADE?

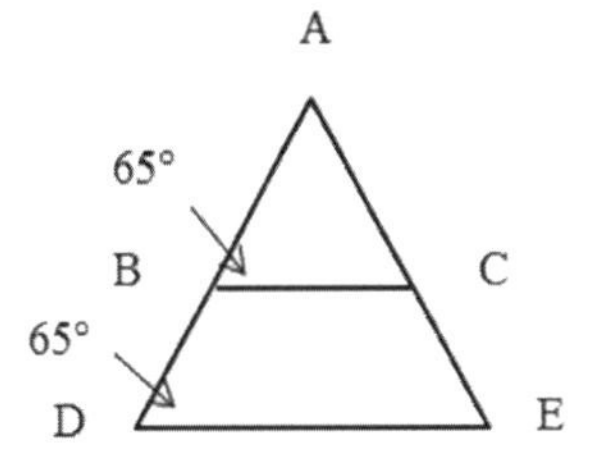

a. ASA
b. AA
c. SAS
d. SSS

7. Students are given the following algebra problem: $2x + 5 = 20$. One student comes up with an answer of $x = 12.5$. Is the student correct? If not, what has the student most likely done wrong?

a. Yes, the student's answer is correct.
b. No, the student has not rounded up to 13.
c. No, the student has probably not divided both sides by 2.
d. No, the student has most likely added 5 to both sides rather than subtracting.

8. Kim's current monthly rent is $800. She is moving to another apartment complex, where the monthly rent will be $1,100. What is the percent increase in her monthly rent amount?

a. 25.5%
b. 27%
c. 35%
d. 37.5%

9. Which of the following represents the graph of $y = (x+2)^2 - 3$?

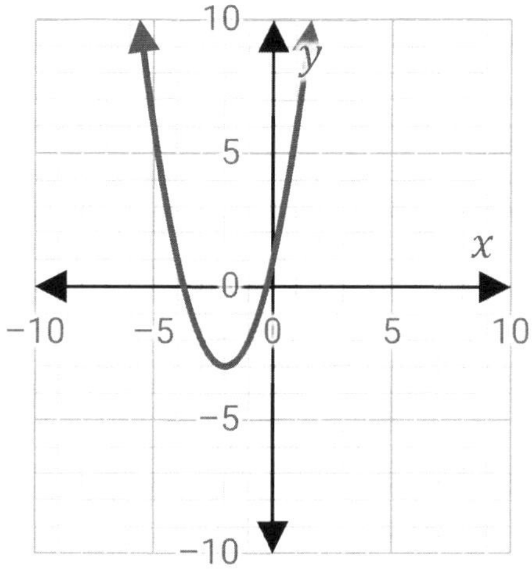

a.

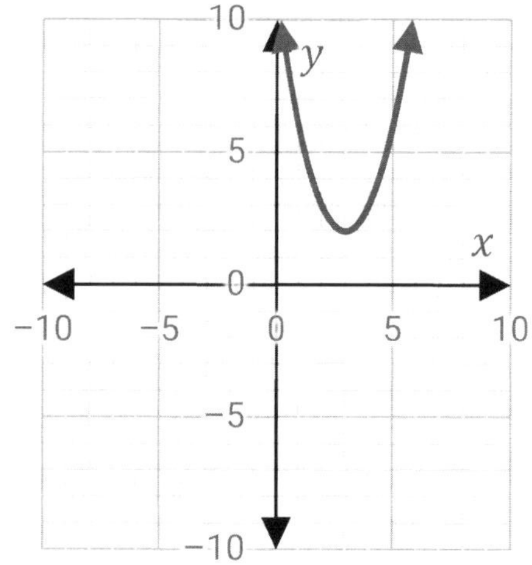

b.

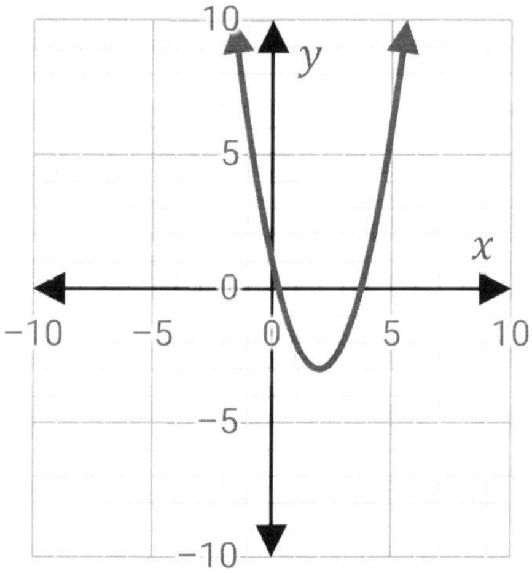

c.

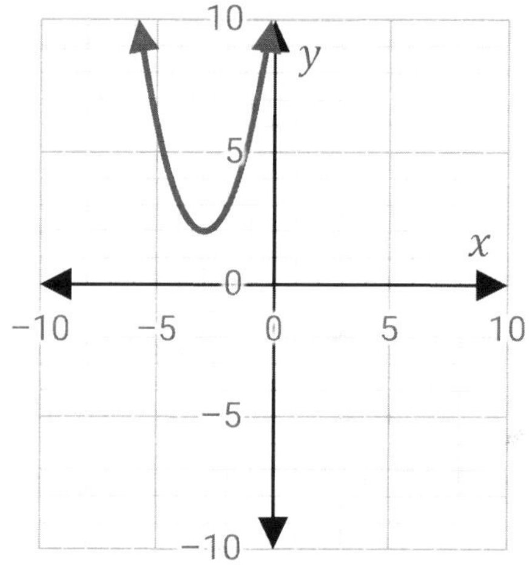

d.

10. Becca needs to order 8 sandwiches for her team lunch, and she knows they will cost at least $40. Which of the following inequalities represents the possible costs?

a. $40 \geq 8s$
b. $40 < 8s$
c. $40 > 8s$
d. $40 \leq 8s$

11. What is $\lim\limits_{n\to\infty} \frac{n-1}{n^2}$?

a. 0
b. 1
c. 2
d. There is no limit.

12. A convex three-dimensional figure has 12 edges and 8 vertices. How many faces does it have?

a. 4
b. 5
c. 6
d. 8

13. Which of the following learning goals is most appropriate for a fourth-grade unit on geometry and measurement?

a. The students will be able to use a protractor to determine the approximate measures of angles in degrees to the nearest whole number.
b. The students will be able to describe the process for graphing ordered pairs of numbers in the first quadrant of the coordinate plane.
c. The students will be able to determine the volume of a rectangular prism with whole number side lengths in problems related to the number of layers times the number of unit cubes in the area of the base.
d. The students will be able to classify two-dimensional figures in a hierarchy of sets and subsets using graphic organizers based on their attributes and properties.

14. The expression $3x^2 + 3x - 18$ is equal to the product of $(x + 3)$ and which other factor?

a. $(3x - 4)$
b. $(3x - 6)$
c. $(3x + 4)$
d. $(3x + 6)$

15. Which of the following represents 2,417?

a. 2.417×10^{-3}
b. 2.417×10^{3}
c. 24.17×10^{3}
d. 2.417×10^{4}

16. Anne rolls a die and tosses a coin. What is the probability she gets a prime number greater than 2 or heads?

a. $\frac{1}{2}$
b. $\frac{2}{3}$
c. $\frac{3}{4}$
d. $\frac{5}{6}$

17. What is the contrapositive of the statement below?

If Lucy wears a scarf, it is winter.

a. If Lucy wears a scarf, it is not winter.
b. If Lucy does not wear a scarf, it is not winter.
c. If it is not winter, Lucy does not wear a scarf.
d. If it is winter, Lucy does not wear a scarf.

18. Mrs. Thomas recently taught her fifth grade students a new math concept that they seemed to understand clearly. However, when she administered a unit test of the material, more than half of the students failed. Mrs. Thomas' first reaction should be to:

a. Give the students another chance to learn the material by re-teaching it the same way as she did the first time
b. Analyze the test and the results to determine whether the assessment was well-designed and fairly administered
c. Review the test results to discover exactly which aspect of the material the students had trouble with
d. Compare her students' test results with the performance of last year's fifth grade class on the same test to see if there is a discrepancy

19. Given the boxplots below, which of the following statements is correct?

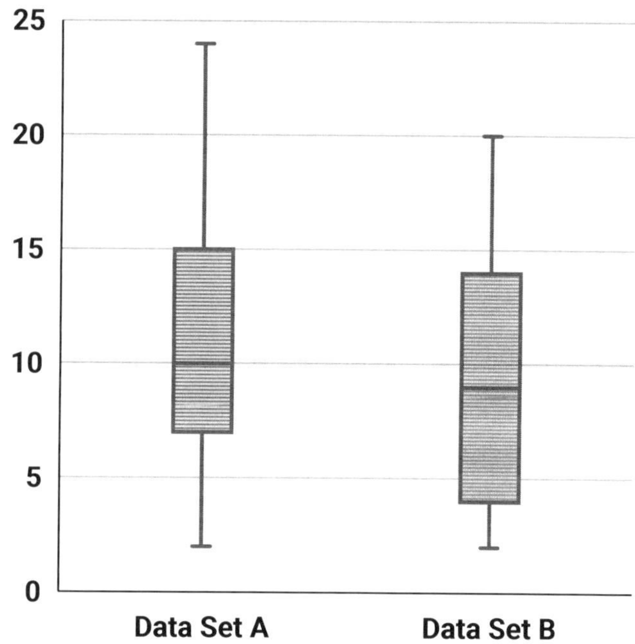

a. Data Set A has a larger range and a larger median.
b. Data Set A has a smaller range and a larger median.
c. Data Set A has a larger range and a smaller median.
d. Data Set A has a smaller range and a smaller median.

20. Which of the following measurements is the best approximation of 2,012 square inches?

a. 11.85 ft^2
b. 12.28 ft^2
c. 13.97 ft^2
d. 15.29 ft^2

21. What scale factor was applied to the smaller triangle to obtain the larger triangle below?

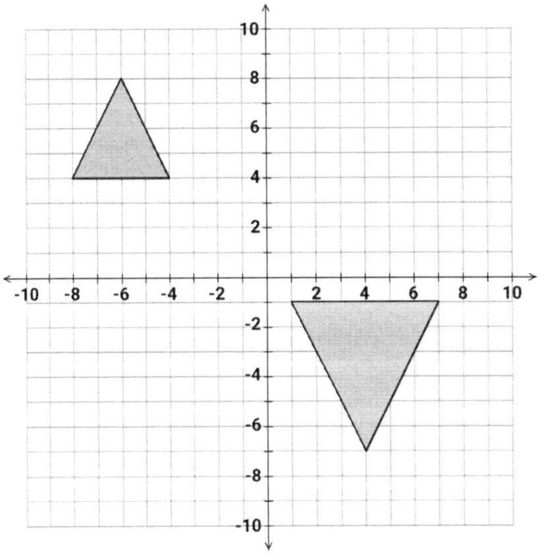

a. $\frac{1}{2}$
b. $\frac{2}{3}$
c. $\frac{3}{2}$
d. $\frac{5}{4}$

22. What is the length of the hypotenuse in the triangle shown below?

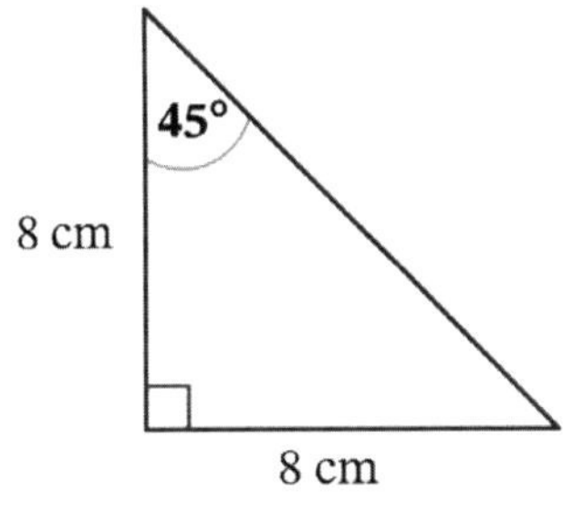

a. 4 cm
b. $8\sqrt{3}$ cm
c. 16 cm
d. $8\sqrt{2}$ cm

23. Which of the following equations represents a line perpendicular to the one graphed below and passing through the point $(3, 2)$?

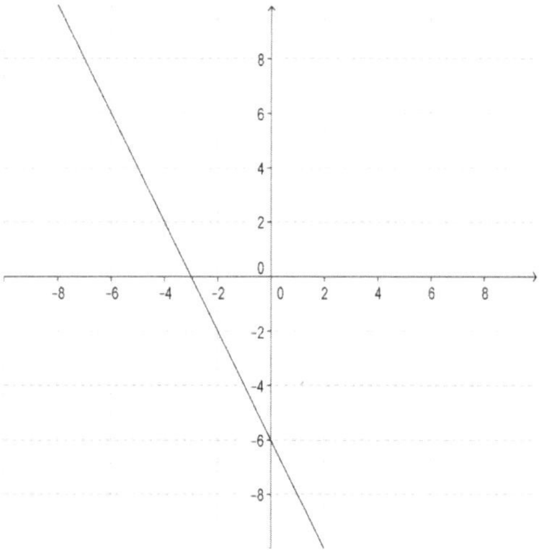

a. $y = \frac{1}{2}x + 2$
b. $y = \frac{1}{2}x + \frac{1}{2}$
c. $y = \frac{3}{2}x + \frac{1}{2}$
d. $y = 2x + 2$

24. Which of the following correctly compares the sets of whole numbers and counting numbers?

a. The sets of whole and counting numbers are equal.
b. The sets of whole and counting numbers are disjoint.
c. The set of whole numbers is a subset of the set of counting numbers.
d. The set of counting numbers is a subset of the set of whole numbers.

25. The total amount Carlos has spent on his rent is represented by the graph below. The x-axis represents the number of months since he began his lease, and the y-axis represents the total cost ($500 deposit plus $750 per month). What is the relationship between the total cost and the number of months?

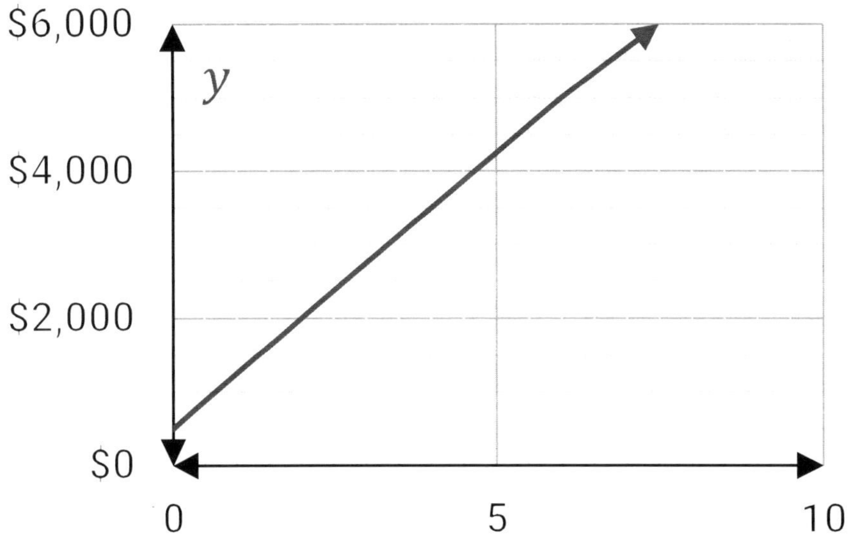

a. The cost is linear, but not proportional.
b. The cost is linear and proportional.
c. The cost is proportional, but not linear.
d. The cost represents an inverse proportional relationship.

26. Which of the following assessment methods is most likely to be used in a learner-centered classroom?

a. A method that provides different alternatives for students to demonstrate their knowledge
b. A method that allows students to complete the assessment in groups
c. A structured method that allows students' mastery to be compared with that of other students
d. A multiple-choice test which students help to construct and grade

27. Which of the following represents a function?

a. $\{(2,9), (3,5), (6,8), (-1,-6), (3,-2)\}$
b. $\{(8,8), (7,9), (2,1), (8,3), (3,6)\}$
c. $\{(-4,6), (2,4), (-4,-2), (3,5), (9,2)\}$
d. $\{(2,6), (6,5), (5,9), (1,0), (-3,1)\}$

28. Which of the following steps were applied to ΔABC?

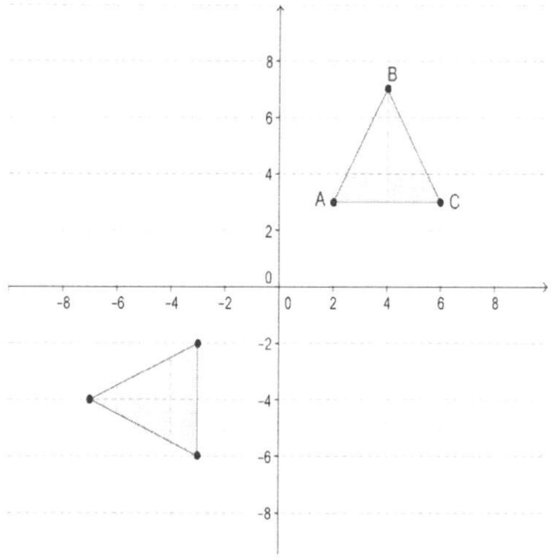

a. Reflection across the x-axis and counterclockwise rotation of 90 degrees about the origin
b. Reflection across the x-axis and counterclockwise rotation of 180 degrees about the origin
c. Reflection across the x-axis and counterclockwise rotation of 270 degrees about the origin
d. Reflection across the y-axis and counterclockwise rotation of 180 degrees about the origin

29. Which of the following pairs of shapes may tessellate a plane?

a. Equilateral triangles and squares
b. Regular pentagons and equilateral triangles
c. Regular pentagons and squares
d. Regular octagons and equilateral triangles

30. Gillian works out for 15 minutes a day for the first month. During each subsequent month, she plans to exercise an additional 5 minutes per day compared to the previous month. Which of the following equations represents the amount she will work out each day during the nth month?

a. $a_n = 15n - 5$
b. $a_n = 15n + 1$
c. $a_n = 5n + 10$
d. $a_n = 5n + 15$

31. Mario makes an offer of $158,400 on a home. This is a markdown of 12% from the asking price. What was the asking price?

a. $175,000
b. $175,550
c. $178,500
d. $180,000

32. Of the following, which use of math skills for everyday situations is most related to a student's application of math for an English class?

a. To determine the value of an unknown number
b. To determine scores needed to get from B to A
c. To determine the area of the school auditorium
d. To determine supplies needed for PTA meeting

33. The best time to introduce a student to subtraction with two-digit numerals is:

a. Before the student reaches the fourth grade
b. When the student has proved proficient in adding long columns of numbers
c. When the student has achieved automatic response to subtraction facts
d. When the student expresses an interest in advancing his or her subtraction skills

34. What is the main purpose of formative assessments?

a. To establish the background knowledge of students prior to beginning a unit
b. To assess students partway through a unit to establish which content is mastered and which needs to be retaught
c. To compare data to other teachers and assess the effectiveness of the teacher
d. To assess students at the conclusion of a unit of study

35. Matt rolls a standard six-sided die. What is the probability he rolls a prime number?

a. $\frac{1}{4}$
b. $\frac{1}{2}$
c. $\frac{2}{3}$
d. $\frac{3}{4}$

36. According to the scatter plot below, which of the following is the *best* estimate for the earnings received for 20 hours of work?

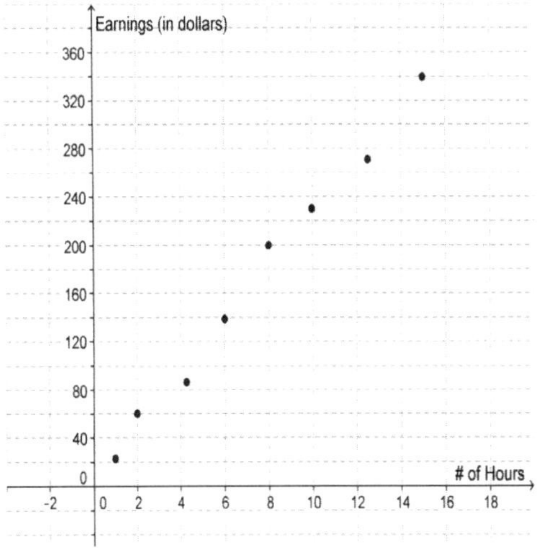

a. \$342
b. \$446
c. \$528
d. \$602

37. What is $\lim\limits_{n \to \infty} \frac{n^2+1}{n}$?

a. 0
b. 1
c. 2
d. There is no limit.

38. What is $\lim_{x \to -2}(3x^3 - 6x^2 + 4)$?

a. −44
b. −42
c. 4
d. 52

39. Which of the following pairs of shapes may tessellate a plane?

a. Regular pentagons and squares
b. Regular pentagons and equilateral triangles
c. Equilateral triangles and regular hexagons
d. Regular octagons and equilateral triangles

40. A class is multiplying whole numbers by fractions. Four of the students correctly responded that $10 \times \frac{3}{5} = 6$. Their teacher asks each student to give his or her reasoning. The students' responses show that each student arrived at his or her answer in a different way. Read the following student explanations and indicate which explanations demonstrate mathematically valid reasoning. Select all that apply.

Student responses	Valid	Invalid
A: "I made $\frac{3}{5}$ into the decimal 0.3 and then multiplied it by 10 and multiplied that by 2."		
B: "I divided 10 by 5, which is 2, and then multiplied it by 3."		
C: "I multiplied 10 by 3, which is 30, and then divided it by 5."		
D: "I drew 10 rectangles and split them all into fifths and colored three fifths in all of them and then regrouped the colored ones to see how many I had."		

41. Mel is purchasing gifts for her students. She wants to buy stickers and notepads. She may purchase a maximum of 25 items and plans to spend at least \$60. Each sheet of stickers costs \$2, and each notepad costs \$3. Which of the following graphs correctly shows the possible combinations of stickers and notepads that she may buy, assuming that the x-axis represents sheets of stickers and the y-axis represents notepads?

a. 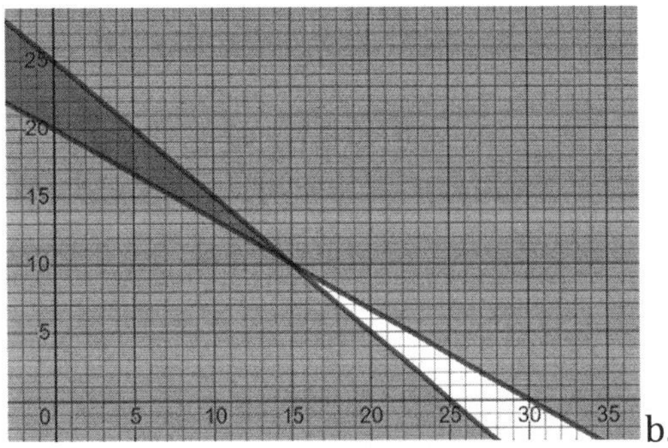

b. 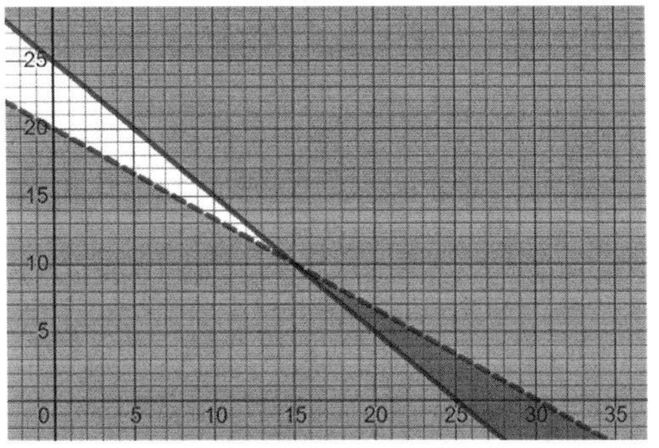

c. 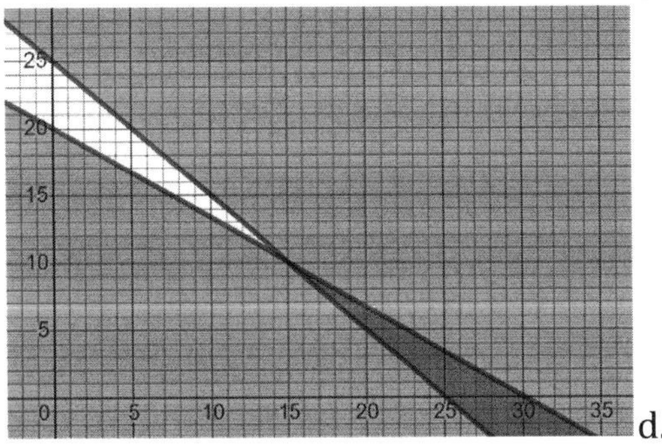

d. 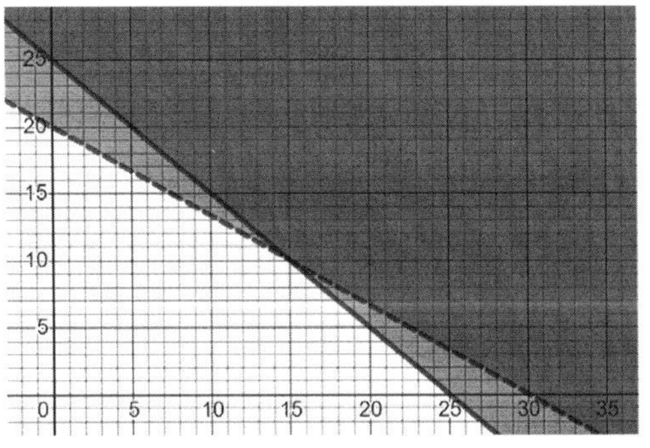

42. Keisha is solving a problem asking her to mix lemonade from a powder mix:

> The instructions on the lemonade label say "To make 8 cups of lemonade, mix 1 cup powder with 8 cups of water". You need 24 cups of lemonade. How much powder should you use?

Keisha writes that she will need 17 cups of lemonade powder. Which teacher prompt best addresses Keisha's error and helps her find the correct answer?

a. "It looks like you multiplied 8 by 2 instead of 3. Let's try multiplying by 3."
b. "It looks like you added 16 cups to both the lemonade powder and the water. Could you instead tell me how many batches of 8 cups you will need to make in order to get 24 cups?"
c. Both (a) and (b)
d. Neither (a) nor (b)

43. Which of the following transformations has been applied to ΔABC?

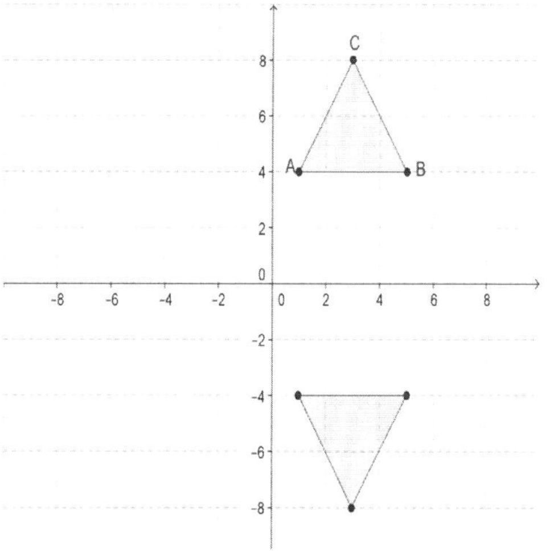

a. Translation
b. Rotation of 90 degrees
c. Reflection
d. Dilation

44. Which of the following correctly represents the expanded form of 0.158?

a. $1 \times \frac{1}{10^0} + 5 \times \frac{1}{10^1} + 8 \times \frac{1}{10^2}$
b. $1 \times \frac{1}{10^1} + 5 \times \frac{1}{10^2} + 8 \times \frac{1}{10^3}$
c. $1 \times \frac{1}{10^3} + 5 \times \frac{1}{10^2} + 8 \times \frac{1}{10^1}$
d. $1 \times \frac{1}{10^2} + 5 \times \frac{1}{10^3} + 8 \times \frac{1}{10^4}$

45. Given the two-way frequency table below, which of the following best represents P(Blue or Felt tip)?

	Felt tip	Ballpoint	Total
Black	3,114	5,283	8,397
Blue	1,756	2,459	4,215
Total	4,870	7,742	12,612

a. 55%
b. 60%
c. 65%
d. 70%

46. Which of the following is an irrational number?

a. $0.\overline{5}$
b. $e + 3$
c. $\frac{41}{3}$
d. $(\sqrt{3})^2$

47. Mr. Martinez is explaining to his students how they can tell if a fraction is less than one, equal to one, or greater than one. Which of the following math vocabulary terms must his students know in order to be able to understand and apply his explanation?

a. Mixed and equivalent
b. Like and unlike
c. Proper and improper
d. Numerator and denominator

48. The first thing students should be encouraged to do when attempting to solve a mathematical word problem is to:

a. Write the appropriate equation
b. List the steps needed to solve the problem
c. Think about what information the problem is asking them to find
d. Compare the problem to similar problems they have solved in the past

49. What is the perimeter of the trapezoid graphed below?

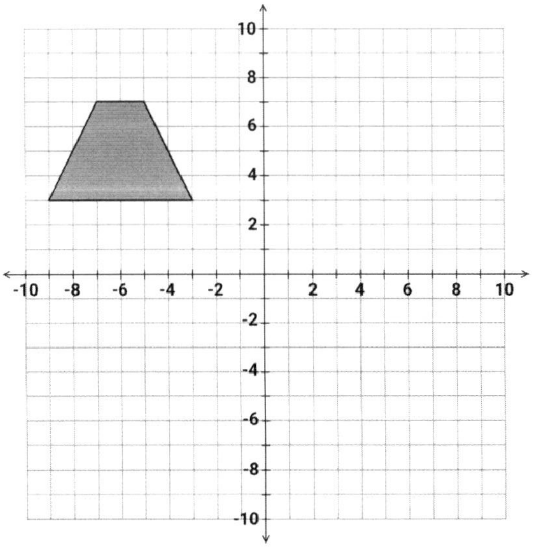

a. $6 + \sqrt{10}$
b. $8 + 4\sqrt{5}$
c. $8 + 2\sqrt{5}$
d. $7 + 2\sqrt{10}$

50. If $f(x) = \frac{2x^3 - 10x + 6}{3x}$, what is $f(3)$?

a. $\frac{10}{3}$
b. 10
c. $\frac{10}{9}$
d. 2

51. For which of the following data sets would the mean be an appropriate measure of center to use?

a. 7, 7, 7, 10, 12, 13, 16, 17, 41, 42
b. 6, 12, 52, 52, 54, 57, 57, 59, 61, 65
c. 5, 8, 9, 9, 13, 16, 18, 19, 21, 21
d. 27, 28, 30, 30, 35, 38, 41, 41, 42, 1786

52. A ball has a diameter of 5 inches. Which of the following best represents the volume?

a. 65.4 in^3
b. 69.6 in^3
c. 72.5 in^3
d. 78.3 in^3

53. Given the boxplots below, which of the following statements is correct? (Note that the boxes are not drawn to scale with one another.)

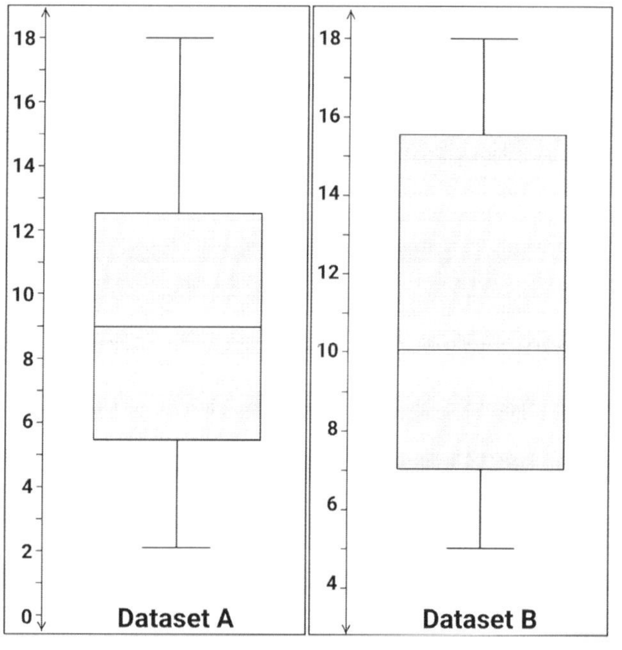

a. Dataset A has a larger range and a larger median.
b. Dataset A has a smaller range and a larger median.
c. Dataset A has a larger range and a smaller median.
d. Dataset A has a smaller range and a smaller median.

54. Which of the following skills do students need in order to solve word problems involving mean and median?

a. Counting, ordering, adding, subtracting, and dividing
b. Counting, adding, and dividing
c. Counting, ordering, adding, and dividing
d. Ordering, adding, and dividing

55. Eric has a beach ball with a radius of 9 inches. He is planning to wrap the ball with wrapping paper. Which of the following is the best estimate for the number of square feet of wrapping paper he will need? Use 3.14 for π.

a. 4.08
b. 5.12
c. 7.07
d. 8.14

56. A gift box has a length of 14 inches, a height of 8 inches, and a width of 6 inches. How many square inches of wrapping paper are needed to wrap the box?

a. 56
b. 244
c. 488
d. 672

57. Regarding the relationship of cognitive problem-solving skills to mathematics, which of these is true?

a. Problem-solving skills inform mathematical thinking but not social skills.
b. Developing problem-solving skills aids math rather than language skills.
c. Students apply logical reasoning to solve every day and novel problems.
d. Children must be taught to have interest in solving everyday problems.

58. What is $\lim_{x\to-\infty} \frac{x}{x^2-4}$?

a. 1
b. $-\frac{1}{4}$
c. 0
d. There is no limit.

59. Which of the following functions converges?

a. $f(x) = \frac{3x^2}{2x}$
b. $f(x) = 12 - \frac{7x^2}{x^2}$
c. $f(x) = 7x$
d. $f(x) = \frac{x^2+2}{x}$

60. Which type of function is represented by the table of values below?

x	y
−2	−4
−1	−0.5
0	0
1	0.5
2	4

a. Linear
b. Quadratic
c. Cubic
d. Exponential

61. Which of the following formulas may be used to represent the sequence 1, 2, 4, 8, 16, ...?

a. $y = 2x$
b. $y = x + 2$
c. $y = 2^{x-1}$
d. $y = x^2$

62. Natasha designs a square pyramidal tent for her children. Each of the sides of the square base measures *x* ft, and the tent's height is *h* feet. If Natasha were to increase by 1 ft the length of each side of the base, how much more interior space would the tent have?

a. $\frac{x^2h+2xh+h}{3}$ ft^3
b. $\frac{2xh+h}{3}$ ft^3
c. $\frac{x^2h+3}{3}$ ft^3
d. 1 ft^3

63. Which of the following correctly represents the expanded form of 0.593?

a. $5 \times \frac{1}{10^0} + 9 \times \frac{1}{10^1} + 3 \times \frac{1}{10^2}$
b. $5 \times \frac{1}{10^2} + 9 \times \frac{1}{10^3} + 3 \times \frac{1}{10^4}$
c. $5 \times \frac{1}{10^3} + 9 \times \frac{1}{10^2} + 3 \times \frac{1}{10^1}$
d. $5 \times \frac{1}{10^1} + 9 \times \frac{1}{10^2} + 3 \times \frac{1}{10^3}$

64. A box has a length of 22 centimeters, a height of 5 centimeters, and a width of 8 centimeters. How many square centimeters of plastic are needed to shrink-wrap the box?

a. 560
b. 652
c. 748
d. 880

65. Julia rolls a standard six-sided die 300 times. How many times can she expect to roll a 6?

a. 50
b. 75
c. 100
d. 125

66. Ms. Grimes knows that her 4th-grade students will be taking standardized tests next month and hopes to prepare them well. She notices during practice testing that the students are struggling with money concepts, particularly the concept of making change. This is not a complete surprise to her, based upon the students' class work. What would be the best way to approach this scenario?

a. Review each question on the practice tests carefully and walk the students through the proper way to do each problem. Deliver the practice test again a few days later to determine if the students' skills have improved.
b. Use test questions and answers from last year's test to practice and memorize
c. Set up a miniature grocery store with real items and packages labeled with prices; allow the students to practice purchasing items at the "store" and making change. Monitor and review practice test questions.
d. Give more lessons on, and review about, adding and subtracting decimals in order to help the students solidify their procedural knowledge. Explain that money concepts are simply word problems that involve decimals.

67. Mr. Tollison has noticed that many of his eighth grade math students are not completing their homework assignments at all, are partially completing them or are completing the wrong problems. Mr. Tollison's first response should be to:

a. Call the students' parents if they fail to turn in more than one assignment
b. Grade whatever problems the students do turn in, even if they are not the right ones
c. Develop a system to ensure that all students correctly record the homework assignment
d. Walk the students through a few of the homework problems before they leave class

68. In a probability unit in eighth grade, a teacher assigns multiple word problems nightly for the students' homework. The students complain that the word problems are boring and that they do not want to do them. What can the teacher do to help the students become more engaged in the probability unit?

a. Excuse the students from homework and only do math problems in class for the remainder of the unit.
b. Teach a lesson on the importance of word problems and how they will relate to everyday life.
c. Ask teachers of other subjects for word problems that can be used in her classroom.
d. Create word problems that better relate to real-world experiences for the students.

69. Students in a second-grade class have just completed an end-of-chapter test on basic multiplication facts. While scoring the assessments, the teacher noticed that many students did not perform well. Therefore, she is planning instruction to reteach foundational skills. Which of the following strategies would be helpful for this teacher to review to develop students' understanding of this concept?

a. Place value
b. Decomposing numbers
c. Counting on
d. Skip counting

70. What is the slope of the hypotenuse in the triangle graphed below?

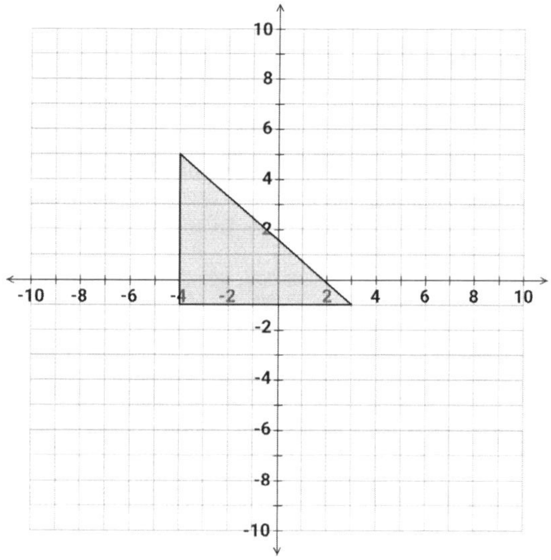

a. $-\frac{6}{7}$
b. $-\frac{7}{6}$
c. $\frac{6}{7}$
d. $\frac{7}{6}$

71. Elijah pays a $30 park entrance fee plus $4 for every ticket he buys. Which of the following equations correctly represents his total cost y in terms of the number of tickets x?

a. $y = 30x + 4$
b. $y = 34x$
c. $y = 4x + 30$
d. $y = 34x + 30$

72. Which of the following best represents the standard deviation of the data below?

23, 24, 26, 28, 31, 32, 35, 35

a. 3.9
b. 4.3
c. 4.7
d. 5.1

73. What linear equation includes the data in the table below?

x	y
−3	1
1	−11
3	−17
5	−23
9	−35

a. $y = -3x - 11$
b. $y = -6x - 8$
c. $y = -3x - 8$
d. $y = -12x - 11$

74. What is the interquartile range of the data below?

$\{1,2,4,8,11,14,14,18,19,23\}$

a. 8
b. 10
c. 12
d. 14

75. What is the best way that a teacher can utilize the data from standardized tests from the previous year?

a. Seat students with similar deficiencies together in class to make it easier to facilitate learning
b. Identify the highest and the lowest achievers and enact a plan for the highest achievers to assist the lowest achievers
c. Identify the achievement gaps of each student and create a plan that addresses the largest gaps
d. Compare data with other teachers in the grade level to evaluate the best methods for instruction

76. How many ways can the 1st–4th place finishers be selected from 7 competitors?

a. 120
b. 360
c. 720
d. 840

77. The initial term of a sequence is 5. Each term in the sequence is $\frac{3}{5}$ the amount of the previous term. What is the sum of the terms, as n approaches infinity?

a. 5
b. 8
c. 12.5
d. 15.75

78. Javier finds a laptop on sale for $450. If it had been marked down 40%, what was the original cost?

a. $800
b. $750
c. $650
d. $600

79. Which of the following correctly represents the expanded form of 0.867?

a. $8 \times \frac{1}{10^0} + 6 \times \frac{1}{10^1} + 7 \times \frac{1}{10^2}$
b. $8 \times \frac{1}{10^2} + 6 \times \frac{1}{10^3} + 7 \times \frac{1}{10^4}$
c. $8 \times \frac{1}{10^3} + 6 \times \frac{1}{10^2} + 7 \times \frac{1}{10^1}$
d. $8 \times \frac{1}{10^1} + 6 \times \frac{1}{10^2} + 7 \times \frac{1}{10^3}$

80. Which expression is represented by the diagram below?

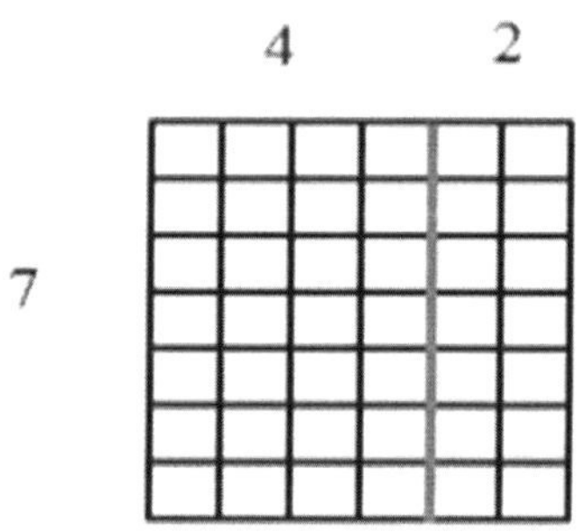

a. $7 + (4 + 2)$
b. $7 \times (4 \times 2)$
c. $7 + (4 \times 2)$
d. $7 \times (4 + 2)$

81. Given the two-way frequency table below, which of the following best represents P(male or graduate)?

	Undergraduate	Graduate	Total
Male	2,940	2,045	4,985
Female	3,026	2,068	5,094
Total	5,966	4,113	10,079

a. 55%
b. 60%
c. 70%
d. 75%

82. Megan rolls a standard six-sided die and tosses a coin. What is the probability she gets a number greater than 5 and tails?

a. $\frac{1}{6}$
b. $\frac{1}{4}$
c. $\frac{1}{8}$
d. $\frac{1}{12}$

83. Which of the following equations represents a line that is parallel to the one graphed below and that passes through the point $(-2, 2)$?

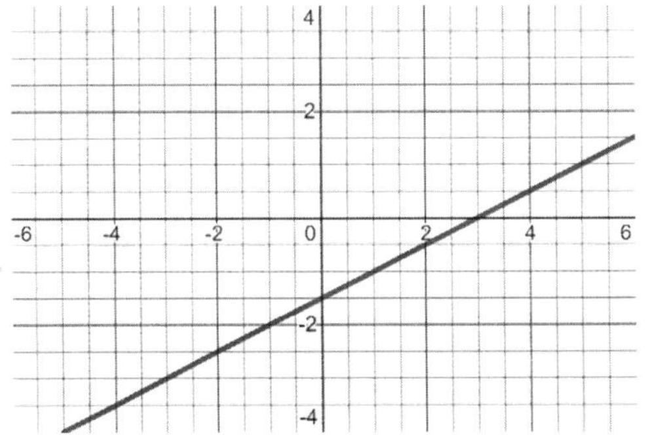

a. $y = \frac{1}{2}x + 3$
b. $y = \frac{1}{2}x - \frac{3}{2}$
c. $y = -2x - 2$
d. $y = -2x - \frac{3}{2}$

84. Four students all love animals equally, but express it differently and have different individual talents. As an example of helping them make informed educational and career decisions, which one should educators encourage to explore pursuing a career as a veterinarian?

a. The student who excels at gentle handling and beautifying but hates math and science
b. The student who excels at and enjoys all subjects in mathematics and in the sciences
c. The student who excels at rescuing and nursing animals and is average in math/science
d. The student who excels at conservation, protecting species, and captive habitat work

85. Will tosses a coin 250 times. How many times can he expect to get tails?

a. 75
b. 100
c. 125
d. 150

86. Which of the following graphs represents the solution to $y \geq 3x - 6$?

a. 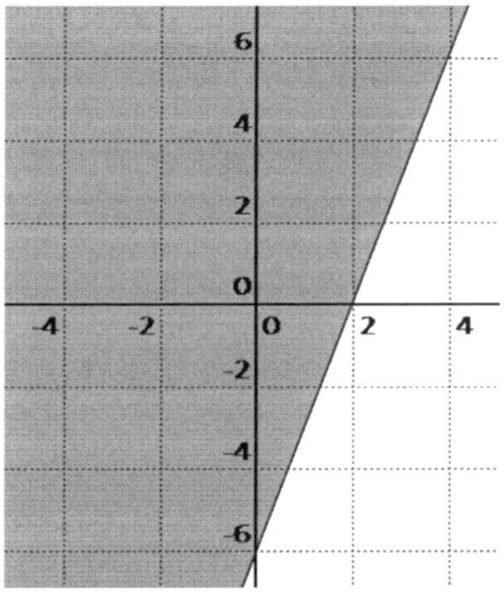

b. 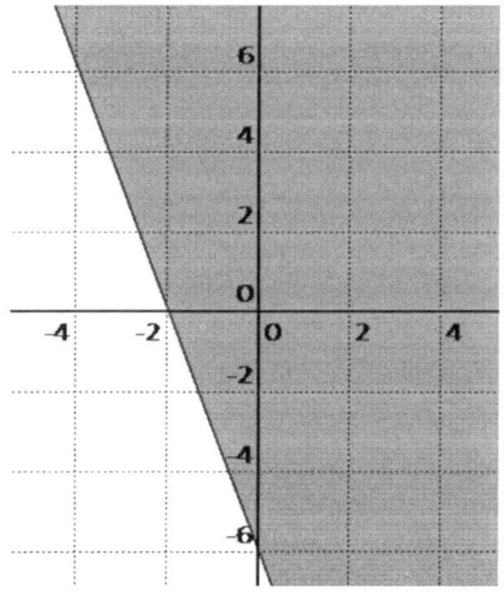

c. 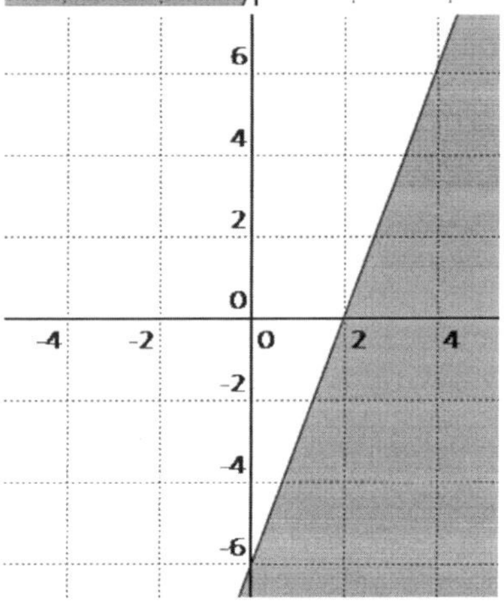

d. 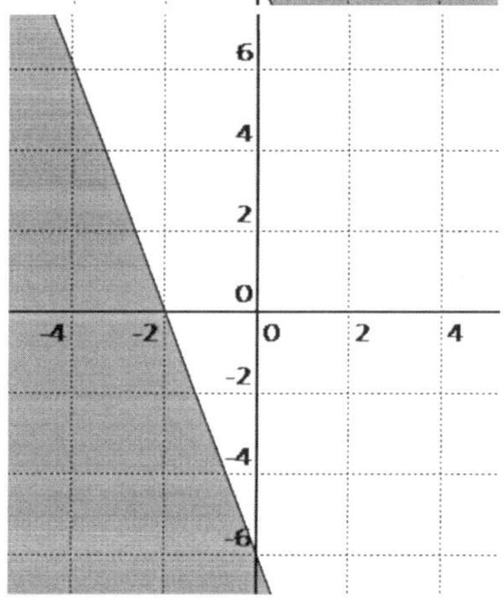

87. Ms. Brooks, a math specialist, is observing a first-year teacher whose learning objective is "Students will use proportional relationships to make an accurate scale model of a backyard." She hears the teacher gives the following explanation:

> "Let's say that the backyard is 60 feet by 30 feet. Obviously we don't have a piece of paper big enough to draw the back yard exactly the size that it is. So, what we are going to do is choose a smaller measurement to represent a foot. If we use an inch to be that smaller measurement, then we need a piece of paper that is 60 inches by 30 inches. But our paper is only 30 inches by 20 inches. Does anyone have a suggestion for what smaller measurement we should use?"

In order for the teacher to meet the learning objective, what should she change about her explanation?

a. Find a different size of paper for the students to use
b. Explain the difference between linear feet and square feet
c. Represent inches as a fraction of a foot
d. Show students the way to write the chosen scale mathematically

88. Robert needs to buy milk and bread. Each gallon of milk costs $3. Each loaf of bread costs $2. He intends to spend at least $20. Which of the following graphs represents the possible combinations of gallons of milk and loaves of bread that he may purchase?

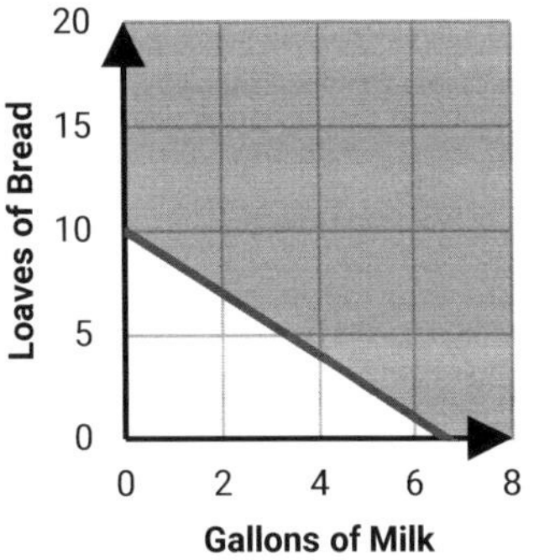

a.

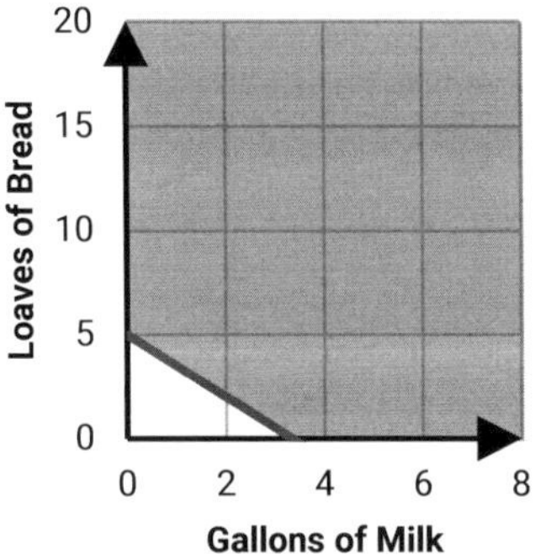

b.

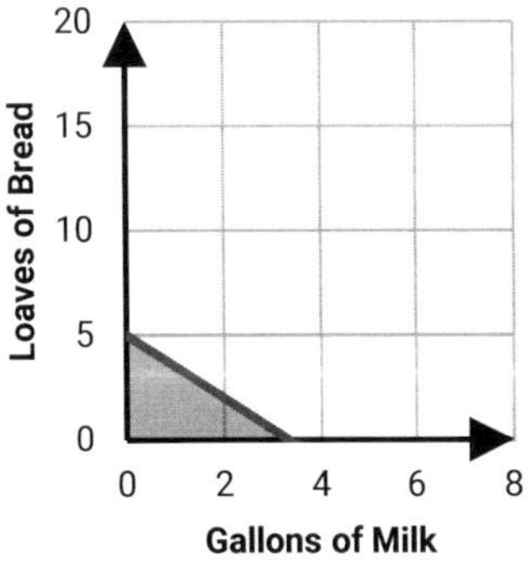

c.

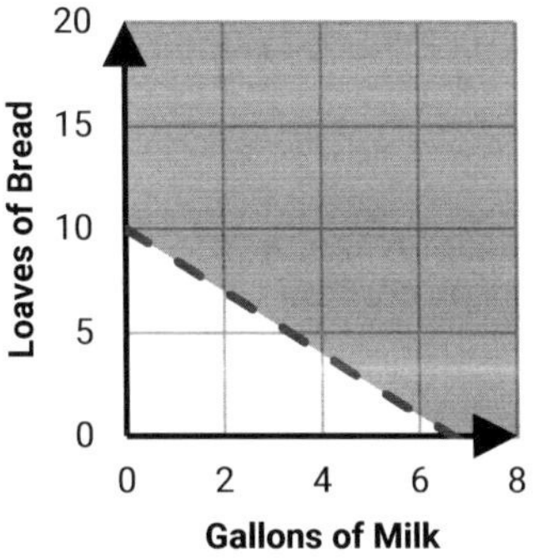

d.

89. Ben's current monthly rent is $750. He is moving to another apartment complex, where the monthly rent will be $900. What is the percent increase in his monthly rent amount?

a. 15%
b. 17.5%
c. 19.25%
d. 20%

90. How many ways can you arrange the letters below, if order does NOT matter?

PIZZA

a. 30
b. 60
c. 90
d. 120

91. Quentin sets aside 10% of his monthly salary to save for a car. If his monthly salary is $2,450, how much will he set aside each month?

a. $2.45
b. $24.50
c. $245
d. $2,450

92. What scale factor was applied to the larger triangle to obtain the smaller triangle below?

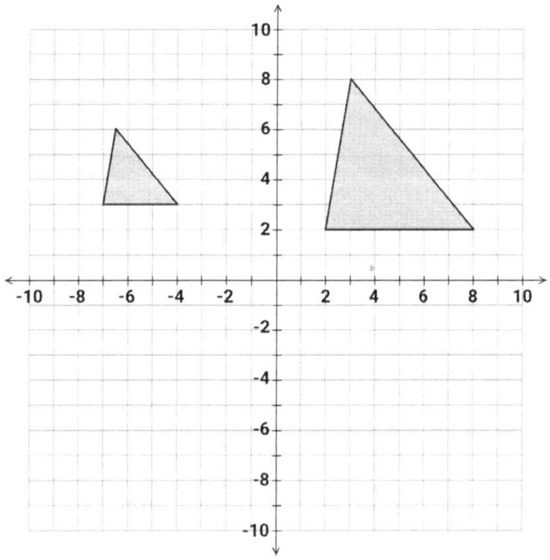

a. $\frac{1}{4}$
b. $\frac{1}{3}$
c. $\frac{1}{2}$
d. $\frac{2}{3}$

93. What is the size of the sample space for flipping a coin five times?

a. 8
b. 16
c. 32
d. 64

94. If the x-axis in the scatter plot below represents the number of items sold and the y-axis represents the total profit in dollars, which of the following is the best estimate for the profit received for selling 15 items?

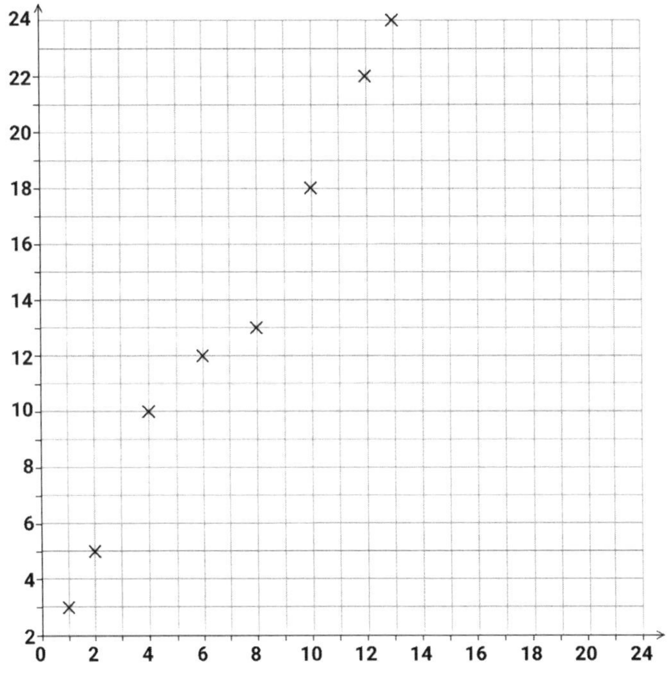

a. $24
b. $27
c. $30
d. $33

95. What is the contrapositive of the statement below?

If Bryan eats peanuts, he has an allergic reaction.

a. If Bryan eats peanuts, he does not have an allergic reaction.
b. If Bryan does not have an allergic reaction, he does not eat peanuts.
c. If Bryan does not eat peanuts, he does not have an allergic reaction.
d. If Bryan does not eat peanuts, he has an allergic reaction.

96. A teacher is working on improving organizational skills with her students. She allows five minutes of time at the end of every class for students to record what they were working on carefully into their notebooks and update their student planners with any homework or test information. What is the primary function of this strategy?

a. It conveys her expectations that students will be held accountable while in her classroom.
b. It helps to make students aware of which skills need more improvement.
c. It helps teach important life skills that will hopefully lead to increased academic success.
d. It demonstrates to her students that her classroom is a place where they should feel safe to learn.

97. Robert buys a car for $24,210. The price of the car has been marked down by 10%. What was the original price of the car?

a. $25,900
b. $26,300
c. $26,900
d. $27,300

98. Eli rolls a six-sided die and tosses a coin. What is the probability that he gets a prime number or tails?

a. $\frac{1}{4}$

b. $\frac{1}{3}$

c. $\frac{1}{2}$

d. $\frac{3}{4}$

99. Which of the following illustrates the additive inverse property?

a. The sum of a and 0 is a.
b. The sum of a and $-a$ is 0.
c. The sum of a and a is $2a$.
d. The sum of a and any variable x is $a + x$.

100. What is the slope of the leg marked x in the triangle graphed below?

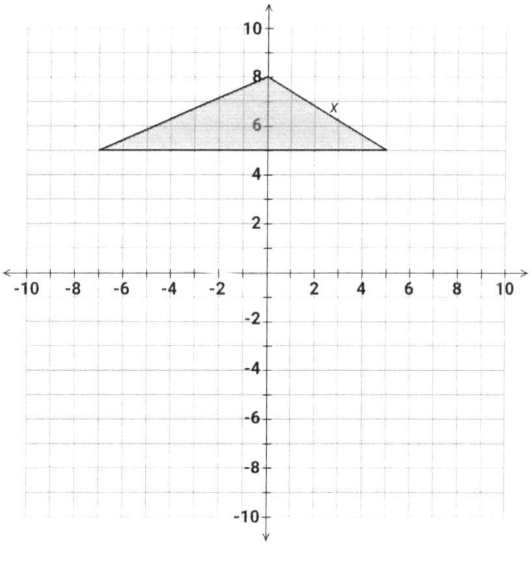

a. -3

b. $-\frac{3}{5}$

c. $\frac{3}{5}$

d. 3

Constructed Response

1. Shawna buys a new motorcycle for a purchase price of \$9,800. The motorcycle will lose 20% of its value the day it is purchased and it will depreciate at a constant rate following that. The value of the motorcycle as a function of time can be modeled by $y = m - 0.08mx$, where y is the value of the motorcycle x years after it was purchased and m is the value after the initial 20% depreciation.

Part A: What is the value of the motorcycle 4 years after its purchase date? Show your work.

Part B: On an xy-grid, graph the value, y, of the motorcycle, as a function of x, where x represents the number of years after the purchase date, for $0 \leq x \leq 6$ years. Label the axes and show the scales used for the graph.

Part C: Use your graph to estimate the number of years, x, after the purchase date that the value of the motorcycle is \$6,000. Label this point on your graph and indicate the approximate coordinates of the point.

Part D: Algebraically find the number of years, x, after the purchase date that the value of the motorcycle is exactly \$6,000. Round your solution to the nearest tenth of a year. Show your work.

2. The diagram below shows a city square, where the city is installing new lights. The circles in the diagram show the areas that will be illuminated by the new lights. Each of the border lights has an illumination diameter of 12 feet and the center light has a diameter of 15 feet. The square has a diagonal of 80 feet.

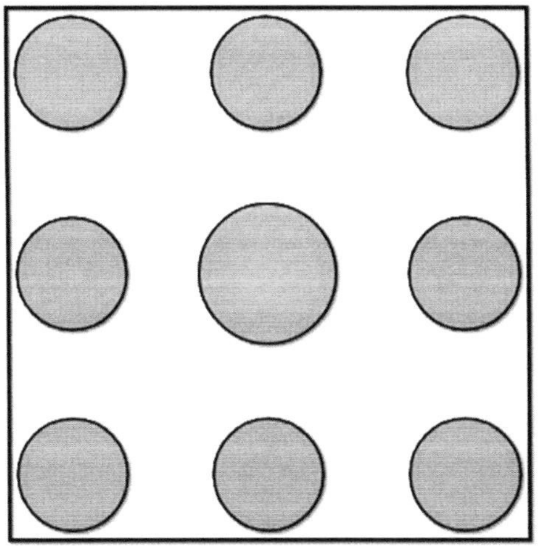

Part A: According to the diagram, what is the area that will be illuminated by the new lights? Show your work.

Part B: According to the diagram, what percentage of the square will NOT be illuminated by the new lights? Show your work.

Part C: If a ball were to fall on a random point within the square, what is the probability that the ball would fall in an illuminated area? Show your work or explain your reasoning.

3. Below are listed the final grades of the 18 students in a class.

63, 71, 75, 78, 78, 80, 82, 83, 83, 86, 87, 89, 89, 91, 91, 93, 94, 99

Part A: For the numbers above, define and identify the median and the range.

Part B: Draw a stem and leaf plot of the data using the tens digits as the stems and the units digits as the leaves.

Part C: Define and calculate the mean for the list of numbers above.

Answer Key and Explanations for Test #2

Multiple Choice

1. C: Myles needs to purchase a combined total of at least 15 sandwiches and salads, so $x + y \geq 15$. Each sandwich costs \$3, each salad costs \$5, and he has a budget of \$60, so $3x + 5y \leq 60$. Therefore, the system of inequalities is:

$$\begin{cases} x + y \geq 15 \\ 3x + 5y \leq 60 \end{cases}$$

Graph the two lines. They should both be solid lines since both expressions allow equality (i.e., we have $\geq$ and $\leq$ rather than $>$ or $<$). The first inequality should be shaded above the line because he needs to buy 15 or more items, and the second inequality should be shaded below the line because he needs to spend \$60 or less. The overlapping shading occurs in the lower-right portion between the lines, which matches graph C.

2. C: The number 589 can be estimated to be 600. The number 9 can be estimated to be 10. The number of chicken nuggets is approximately 600×10, which is 6,000 nuggets. Therefore, the correct choice is (C).

3. D: The triangle is a 45-45-90 right triangle. If each leg is represented by x, the hypotenuse is then represented by $x\sqrt{2}$. Thus, the hypotenuse is equal to $12\sqrt{2}$ in.

4. B: The midpoint may be calculated by using the formula $m = \left(\frac{x_1+x_2}{2}, \frac{y_1+y_2}{2}\right)$. Thus, the midpoint of the line segment shown may be written as $m = \left(\frac{-5+7}{2}, \frac{-3+5}{2}\right)$, which simplifies to $m = (1, 1)$.

5. D: The Pythagorean theorem may be used to find the diagonal distance from the top of the building to the base of the shadow. The following equation may be written and solved for c: $44^2 + 59.2^2 = c^2$. Thus, $c \approx 73.8$. The distance is approximately 73.8 ft.

6. B: The two triangles are similar because they each have an angle measuring 65°, and the measurement of $\angle A$ is the same for both triangles, due to the Reflexive Property. So the two triangles are similar according to the AA (Angle-Angle) Similarity Postulate.

7. D: The student's answer is incorrect, most likely because the student has added rather than subtracted 5 to both sides. When solving a simple algebraic equation of this type, the goal is to isolate the variable on one side. This is done by eliminating the other terms and coefficients one by one. The most common first step in this problem would be to eliminate the 5 by subtracting an equal amount from both sides of the equation. This would leave $2x = 15$, which leads to the correct solution $x = 7.5$. If 5 was added, however, the resulting equation would be $2x = 25$, which would lead to the student's incorrect answer.

8. D: This problem can be solved using the percent change formula: $\%\ change = \frac{new-old}{old} \times 100\%$. Thus, the percentage increase is represented as $\%\ change = \frac{1{,}100-800}{800} \times 100\% = 37.5\%$.

9. A: Compare the equation $y = (x + 2)^2 - 3$ with its parent function, $y = x^2$. Replacing x with $(x + 2)$ moves the parent function 2 units to the left. Subtracting 3 moves the function 3 units down. Graph A is shifted 2 units left and 3 units down.

10. D: Since she spends at least \$40, the relation of the number of sandwiches to the minimum cost may be written as $8s \geq 40$. Alternatively, the inequality may be written as $40 \leq 8s$.

11. A: If we divide both terms in the numerator by n^2, the expression reduces to $\frac{1}{n} - \frac{1}{n^2}$. Both $\frac{1}{n}$ and $\frac{1}{n^2}$ converge to 0, so the expression can be written as $0 - 0 = 0$. Thus, the limit is 0.

12. C: The relationship between number of faces, edges, and vertices is represented by Euler's Formula, $E = F + V - 2$. Substituting 12 for E and 8 for V gives: $12 = F + 8 - 2$, which simplifies to $12 = F + 6$. Thus, $F = 6$.

13. A: Choice (A) is correct because standards for fourth grade state that students will be able to use a protractor to determine the approximate measures of angles in degrees to the nearest whole number. Choices (B), (C), and (D) are stated in the standards for fifth grade.

14. B: The product of $(x + 3)(3x - 6)$ equals $3x^2 - 6x + 9x - 18$, which simplifies to $3x^2 + 3x - 18$.

15. B: The decimal point is 3 places to the right of the first digit, 2. Thus, $2{,}417 = 2.417 \times 10^3$.

16. B: Since they are not mutually exclusive events, the probability may be written as $P(P \text{ or } H) = P(P) + P(H) - P(P \text{ and } H)$. Because the events are independent, $P(P \text{ and } H) = P(P) \times P(H)$. Substituting the probability of each event gives $(P \text{ or } H) = \frac{1}{3} + \frac{1}{2} - \left(\frac{1}{3} \times \frac{1}{2}\right)$, or $\frac{2}{3}$.

17. C: If the statement is written in the form $p \rightarrow q$, then the contrapositive is represented as $\neg q \rightarrow \neg p$. Thus, the contrapositive should read, "If it is not winter, Lucy does not wear a scarf."

18. B: In order to identify and resolve the problem, Mrs. Thomas' first step should be to consider whether there may be a problem with the assessment itself. Perhaps the assessment did not directly test the material that was covered, or perhaps the students were not given adequate time to complete the assessment. Only if Mrs. Thomas finds no problems with the test itself should she analyze the results to find out exactly which aspects of the material the students struggled with.

19. A: The ends of Data Set A are farther apart, indicating a larger range. The horizontal line in the middle of a boxplot represents the median, so Data Set A also has a larger median.

20. C: Since there are 144 square inches in 1 square foot, the following proportion may be written and solved for x: $\frac{144}{1} = \frac{2{,}012}{x}$. $144x = 2{,}012$. Dividing both sides of the equation by 144 gives $x \approx 13.97$. Thus, 2,012 square inches is approximately equal to 13.97 square feet.

21. C: The smaller triangle has a base length of 4 units and a height of 4 units. The larger triangle has a base length of 6 units and a height of 6 units. Using the base lengths, the dimensions of the smaller triangle were multiplied by a scale factor of $\frac{6}{4}$, which reduces to $\frac{3}{2}$.

22. D: The triangle is a 45-45-90 right triangle. Thus, if each leg is represented by x, the hypotenuse is represented by $x\sqrt{2}$. Thus, the hypotenuse is equal to $8\sqrt{2}$ cm.

23. B: The slope of the graphed line is −2. A line perpendicular to this one will have a slope of $\frac{1}{2}$. Substituting the slope and the x- and y-values from the point (3,2), into the slope-intercept form of an equation gives: $2 = \frac{1}{2}(3) + b$, which simplifies to $2 = \frac{3}{2} + b$. Subtracting $\frac{3}{2}$ from each side of the equation gives $b = \frac{1}{2}$. So, the equation of a line perpendicular to this one and passing through the point (3,2) is $y = \frac{1}{2}x + \frac{1}{2}$.

24. D: The set of whole numbers is represented as $\{0, 1, 2, 3, \ldots\}$. The set of counting numbers is represented as $\{1, 2, 3, \ldots\}$. Thus, the set of whole numbers includes all counting numbers plus zero, so the set of counting numbers is a subset of the set of whole numbers.

25. A: The graph is a straight line, so it is linear. If there were no deposit, the total cost would also be proportional to the number of months ($750 per month). But because the total cost is increased by the one-time $500 deposit, it is not proportional to the number of months.

26. A: Learner-centered assessment provides alternatives that allow different students to be assessed differently. Although student participation in assessment creation (D) is also an important part of learner-centered assessment, a multiple choice test does not reflect the goals of learner-centered assessment because it does not provide an authentic assessment experience.

27. D: Relation D is the only one in which there is not any x-value that is mapped to more than one y-value. Thus, this relation represents a function.

28. C: A reflection across the x-axis will result in a triangle with vertices at $(2, -3)$, $(4, -7)$, and $(6, -3)$. A rotation of 270 degrees counterclockwise is denoted by the following: $(x, y) \rightarrow (y, -x)$. Thus, a rotation of the reflected triangle by 270 degrees will result in a figure with vertices at $(-3, -2)$, $(-7, -4)$, and $(-3, -6)$. The transformed triangle indeed has these coordinates as its vertices.

29. A: Equilateral triangles and squares may tessellate a plane. Each triangle may be attached to each side of a square, leaving no gaps in the plane.

30. C: This situation may be modeled by an arithmetic sequence, with a common difference of 5 and an initial value of 15. Substituting the common difference and initial value into the formula, $a_n = a_1 + (n - 1)d$, gives $a_n = 15 + (n - 1)5$, which simplifies to $a_n = 5n + 10$.

31. D: The original price may be represented by the equation $158{,}400 = x - 0.12x$ or $158{,}400 = 0.88x$. Dividing both sides of the equation by 0.88 gives $x = 180{,}000$.

32. B: A student could apply math to choice (A) most for an algebra class, or any other situation wherein some numbers are known but one is not. For an English class, a student could apply math most to determine what scores are needed to raise a "B" grade to an "A." A student could apply math to choice (C) most for planning attendance at a school play, assembly, or other event using the auditorium space; and to choice (D) for planning to furnish refreshments, seating, forms/paper, pens, etc. at a PTA meeting.

33. C: A student is not ready to solve more complex subtraction problems until he or she has mastered all the single-digit subtraction facts. Grade level, proficiency in addition, and the desire to move ahead are not sufficient indications of the student's readiness.

34. B: The purpose of formative assessments is to assess students partway through a unit to see which parts of the units the students have mastered, as well as which parts of the unit may need to be retaught. These learning checks give the teacher a chance to see how the class is doing and how each student is doing individually. Formative assessments can be given in a variety of manners, including quizzes, tickets out the door, short essays or paragraphs explaining what was learned, as well as multiple other methods.

35. B: The probability of rolling a prime number (2, 3, or 5), denoted $P(Q)$, may be written as $P(Q) = \frac{1}{6} + \frac{1}{6} + \frac{1}{6} = \frac{1}{2}$.

36. B: The points may be entered into a graphing calculator or Excel spreadsheet to find the least-squares regression line. This line is approximately $y = 22x + 6$. Substituting 20 for x gives $y = 22(20) + 6$, or $y = 446$. Thus, \$446 is a good estimate for the earnings received after 20 hours of work. If a line of best fit is predicted visually, the slope between points near that line is around 20, and the line passes near the origin. Thus, another good estimate would be \$400. The estimate of \$446 is closer to \$400 than any of the other choices.

37. D: If we divide both terms in the numerator by n, the expression reduces to $n + \frac{1}{n}$. Although $\frac{1}{n}$ converges to 0, n increases without bound. The expression therefore has no limit.

38. A: Evaluation of the expression for an x-value of −2 gives: $(3(-2)^3 - 6(-2)^2 + 4)$, which equals −44.

39. C: Equilateral triangles and regular hexagons may tessellate a plane. Each triangle may be attached to each side of a hexagon, leaving no gaps in the plane.

40. B, C, D: Choices B and C both use correct order of operations to solve the problem. Choice D is an accurate visual representation of the problem. In choice A, the student inaccurately converted $\frac{3}{5}$ to the decimal 0.3 and did not explain why he or she multiplied by 2 at the end.

41. A: The situation may be modeled by the following system of inequalities: $\begin{cases} 2x + 3y \geq 60 \\ x + y \leq 25 \end{cases}$. A test point of (0,0) indicates shading should occur above the line for the top equation and below the line for the bottom equation. The overlapped shading occurs in the upper left portion between the lines. Thus, choice A represents the correct combinations of items that Mel may buy.

42. B: This prompt would help Keisha think of how to keep the ratio the same while still making the right amount of lemonade.

43. C: The original triangle was reflected across the x-axis. When reflecting across the x-axis, the x-values of each point remain the same, but the y-values of the points will be opposites.

$$(1,4) \rightarrow (1,-4) \quad (5,4) \rightarrow (5,-4) \quad (3,8) \rightarrow (3,-8)$$

44. B: The 1 is in the tenths place, the 5 in the hundredths place, and the 8 in the thousandths place. Thus, 0.158 is equal to the sum of the product of 1 and $\frac{1}{10}$, the product of 5 and $\frac{1}{100}$, and the product of 8 and $\frac{1}{1{,}000}$.

45. B: The probability may be written as $P(Blue \text{ or } FT) = P(Blue) + P(FT) - P(Blue \text{ and } FT)$. Substituting the probabilities, the following may be written: $P(Blue \text{ or } FT) = \frac{4{,}215}{12{,}612} + \frac{4{,}870}{12{,}612} - \frac{1{,}756}{12{,}612}$, which simplifies to $P(Blue \text{ or } FT) = \frac{7{,}329}{12{,}612}$, or approximately 60%.

46. B: A rational number is any number that can be expressed as a ratio (or fraction) of two integers. A number is rational if and only if its decimal form either terminates or repeats infinitely. Choice A, $0.\overline{5} = 0.555 \ldots$, repeats infinitely, so it is rational. Choice C, $\frac{41}{3}$, is the ratio of the integers 41 and 3, so it is rational. Choice D, $(\sqrt{3})^2 = 3$, has a decimal form that terminates, so it is rational.

However, in choice B, the number $e = 2.71828 \ldots$ is known to be irrational. And $e + 3 = 5.71828 \ldots$ will likewise have infinite, nonrepeating decimal digits, so it must be irrational as well.

47. D: The characteristics of these three groups of fractions depend on how their numerator (the number on the top) and their denominator (the number on the bottom) compare. If the denominator is greater than the numerator, then the fraction is less than 1 (e.g., $\frac{5}{7}$). If the numerator and the denominator are the same, the number is equal to 1 (e.g., $\frac{5}{5}$). If the numerator is greater than the denominator, the number is greater than 1 (e.g., $\frac{7}{5}$).

48. C: The student needs to determine what she is being asked to find out before she can decide what equations or steps are needed to solve the problem. Comparing the problem to others like it may be useful, but it is not the first step in solving the problem.

49. B: The perimeter is equal to the sum of the lengths of the two bases, 6 and 2 units, and the diagonal distances of the other two sides. Using the distance formula, each side length may be represented as $d = \sqrt{2^2 + 4^2} = \sqrt{20} = 2\sqrt{5}$. Thus, the sum of the two sides is equal to $2\sqrt{20}$, or $4\sqrt{5}$. The whole perimeter is equal to $8 + 4\sqrt{5}$.

50. A: Substituting 3 for each x-value gives $f(3) = \frac{2(3)^3-10(3)+6}{3(3)} = \frac{54-30+6}{9} = \frac{30}{9} = \frac{10}{3}$.

51. C: Data sets A and B are asymmetrical: data set A is skewed toward lower values, and data set B is skewed toward higher values. This makes the mean a poor measure of center. Data set D is mostly symmetrical, but has a large outlier. The mean is very sensitive to outliers, and is not an appropriate measure of center for data sets that include them. Data set C is roughly symmetrical and has no outliers; the mean would be an appropriate measure of center here.

52. A: The volume of a sphere may be calculated using the formula $V = \frac{4}{3}\pi r^3$, where r represents the radius. Substituting 2.5 for r gives $V = \frac{4}{3}\pi(2.5)^3$, which simplifies to $V \approx 65.4$.

53. C: The ends of Dataset A are farther apart (from 2 to 18 instead of 5 to 18), indicating a larger range. The horizontal line in the middle of a boxplot represents the median, so Dataset A has a smaller median (9 instead of 10).

54. C: To find a mean, students must be able to add the data points, count the number of data points, and divide the sum of the data points by the number of data points. To find a median, students must be able to order the data points, count the number of data points, and divide the number of data points by two in order to find the midpoint.

55. C: The surface area of a sphere may be calculated using the formula $SA = 4\pi r^2$. Substituting 9 for r and 3.14 for π gives $SA = 4(3.14)(9)^2$, which simplifies to $SA = 1{,}017.36$. So, the surface area of the ball is approximately 1,017.36 square inches. There are twelve inches in a foot, so there are $12^2 = 144$ square inches in a square foot. In order to convert this measurement to square feet, the following proportion may be written and solved for x: $\frac{1}{144} = \frac{x}{1{,}017.36}$. So $x = 7.07$. He needs approximately 7.07 square feet of wrapping paper.

56. C: The surface area of a rectangular prism may be calculated using the formula $SA = 2lw + 2wh + 2hl$. Substituting the dimensions of 14 inches, 6 inches, and 8 inches gives $SA = 2(14)(6) + 2(6)(8) + 2(8)(14)$. Thus, the surface area is 488 square inches.

57. C: Students apply logical reasoning to solve both usual, everyday problems and unusual, novel problems they encounter. Developing problem-solving skills not only helps students to think mathematically; it also develops their social skills (A) and language skills (B) when they collaborate to solve problems in math questions, in other school subjects, and in real life; and when they communicate, compare, and discuss their solutions. Children are naturally curious about how everyday problems can be solved: rather than having to teach them this interest (D), teachers can take advantage of this naturally existing motivation by asking them to propose problems; to propose solutions to problems and explain how they reached them; and asking questions about problems and solutions.

58. C: As x goes to positive or negative infinity, only the leading term of a polynomial function of x matters. Therefore, we can ignore the "–4" in the denominator; $\lim_{x\to-\infty} \frac{x}{x^2-4} = \lim_{x\to-\infty} \frac{x}{x^2} = \lim_{x\to-\infty} \frac{1}{x}$. As x goes to negative infinity, $\frac{1}{x}$ approaches zero. The limit is therefore 0.

59. B: The limit of the expression $\frac{7x^2}{x^2}$, is 7, so the limit of the entire function is $12 - 7 = 5$. The function converges.

60. C: The points in table represent a nonlinear curve that rises toward the origin, levels off as it crosses, and then rises again. This is a cubic function.

61. C: The ratio between successive terms is constant (2), so this is a geometric sequence. A geometric sequence is represented by an exponential function. The y-value in this formula represents the value shown in the sequence. The x-value in this formula represents the position of the value in the sequence. For example, the value 4 is the third term in the sequence. Therefore, the x-value is equal to 3. $y = 2^{(3-1)} = 2^2 = 4$. This is the only formula shown that can be applied to the sequence given. Answer choice A is not correct since it represents a linear pattern. If this pattern was used, the first value in the sequence would be 2 instead of 1, since $2(1) = 2$. Answer choice B also represents a linear pattern. If this pattern was used, the first value in the sequence would be 3 instead of 1, since $(1) + 2 = 3$. Thus, choice B is not correct. Answer choice D does represent an exponential function, but the values do not match the pattern in the sequence given. If this pattern was used, the first values match, but the second value would be 4 instead of 2, since $2^2 = 4$. Therefore, answer choice D is also incorrect.

62. B: The volume of Natasha's tent can be found by using the volume formula for a square pyramid, $V = \frac{1}{3}Bh = \frac{1}{3}s^2h$, where B is the area of the base, s is the side length of the square base, and h is the height of the pyramid. Therefore, the volume of her tent is $\frac{x^2h}{3}$. If she were to increase the length of each side of the square base by 1 ft, the tent's volume would be $\frac{(x+1)^2h}{3} = \frac{(x^2+2x+1)(h)}{3} = \frac{x^2h+2xh+h}{3} = \frac{x^2h}{3} + \frac{2xh+h}{3}$. Notice this is the volume of Natasha's tent, $\frac{x^2h}{3}$, increased by $\frac{2xh+h}{3}$.

63. D: The 5 is in the tenths place, the 9 in the hundredths place, and the 3 in the thousandths place. Thus, 0.593 is equal to the sum of the product of 5 and $\frac{1}{10}$, the product of 9 and $\frac{1}{100}$, and the product of 3 and $\frac{1}{1,000}$.

64. B: The surface area of a rectangular prism may be calculated using the formula $SA = 2lw + 2wh + 2hl$. Substituting the dimensions of 22 centimeters, 5 centimeters, and 8 centimeters gives $SA = 2(22)(8) + 2(8)(5) + 2(5)(22)$. Thus, the surface area is 652 square inches.

65. A: The theoretical probability is $\frac{1}{6}$, and $\frac{1}{6}(300) = 50$.

66. C: Students often struggle with money, even though it is a familiar and real-world concept, because there are multiple aspects to consider. In order to do these problems accurately, students must be able to add and subtract decimals. However, they must also understand the practical applications of this concept in their lives. Choices A and B both use test material that will improve this skill without addressing the concept itself. Students need to understand how to make change in the "real world," as well as how to complete a word problem on a test. Choice C addresses the money on a conceptual level in a fun way, combined with monitoring test practice to make sure the students are translating this knowledge to this context. Choice D only addresses one aspect of this issue, without connecting the interrelated skills in a meaningful way.

67. C: Before punishing the students or assuming that they don't understand the material, Mr. Tollison should ensure that all of the students know what the homework assignment is and correctly record it before leaving the classroom. Students may not complete the assignment correctly if they fail to write it down, especially if the assigned problems are shouted out hastily at the end of class.

68. D: When students continually show that they are not engaged in their assignments, teachers should make every effort possible to make the content more relevant to the students. A good way to do this is to create problems and assignments that better relate to the real world the students are experiencing. If they can personally connect to the material, they are more likely to see the value in the assignment. Excusing students from homework for the unit is not a realistic scenario, and teaching a lesson about the importance of word problems is not likely to be an engaging lesson that the students will connect with. While getting other teachers' input can be helpful when designing lessons and problems, the most direct way to improve engagement is to make the word problems relate to the real-world experiences of the students.

69. D: Summative assessments are administered at the end of an instructional unit to evaluate students' mastery of learning objectives. In mathematics instruction, these assessments provide teachers with feedback regarding areas of individual or whole-class need to plan future instruction and determine the need for reteaching specific skills. In this situation, the fact that many students in the class did not perform well on a summative assessment focused on basic multiplication facts indicates the need for whole-class reteaching of foundational skills. One such skill that would be beneficial to review includes skip counting. Skip counting refers to a strategy for counting in ascending order in specific intervals, such as by twos, fives, or tens. Reteaching this concept promotes students' ability to quickly count equal sets of numbers, thus establishing the foundation of understanding necessary to solve basic multiplication problems.

70. A: The slope may be written as $m = \frac{5-(-1)}{-4-3}$, which simplifies to $m = -\frac{6}{7}$.

71. C: Elijah's total cost is \$30 plus \$4 times the number of tickets. Rewriting this in mathematical notation (using y for total cost and x for the number of tickets) gives $y = 30 + 4x$, which is equivalent to choice C.

72. C: The standard deviation is equal to the square root of the ratio of the sum of the squares of the deviation of each score from the mean to the square root of the difference of n and 1. The mean of the data set is 29.25. The deviations are −6.25, −5.25, −3.25, −1.25, 1.75, 2.75, 5.75, and 5.75. The sum of the squares of the deviations may be written as:

$$39.0625 + 27.5625 + 10.5625 + 1.5625 + 3.0625 + 7.5625 + 33.0625 + 33.0625 = 155.5$$

Division of this sum by $n - 1 = 7$ gives 22.21. The square root of this quotient is approximately 4.7.

73. C: Using the points $(-3,1)$ and $(1,-11)$, the slope may be written as $m = \frac{-11-1}{1-(-3)}$ or $m = -3$. Substituting the slope of −3 and the x- and y-values from the point $(-3,1)$, into the slope-intercept form of an equation gives $1 = -3(-3) + b$, which simplifies to $1 = 9 + b$. Subtracting 9 from both sides of the equation gives $b = -8$. Thus, the linear equation that includes the data in the table is $y = -3x - 8$.

74. D: The median of the lower half of the scores is 4. The median of the upper half of the scores is 18. The interquartile range is the difference between the first and third quartiles: $18 - 4 = 14$.

75. C: The best way that a teacher could use standardized test data in her classroom is to use it to analyze gaps in learning that her students may have. They could potentially identify common gaps among the students and identify which students struggled more on specific standards than other students. It allows for the teacher to have an opportunity to plan out what she wants her students to improve upon in the upcoming year and enact a plan to see them achieve.

76. D: This situation describes a permutation, since order matters. The formula for calculating a combination is $P(n,r) = \frac{n!}{(n-r)!}$. This situation may be represented as $P(7,4) = \frac{7!}{(7-4)!}$, which equals 840.

77. C: The sum of an infinite geometric series may be modeled by the formula $S = \frac{a}{1-r}$, where a represents the initial value and r represents the common ratio. Substituting the initial value of 5 and common ratio of $\frac{3}{5}$ into the formula gives $S = \frac{5}{1-\frac{3}{5}}$, which simplifies to $S = \frac{5}{\frac{2}{5}}$ or $\frac{25}{2}$. This can be written as 12.5.

78. B: The original cost may be represented by the equation $\$450 = x - 0.4x$ or $\$450 = 0.6x$. Dividing both sides of the equation by 0.6 gives $x = \$750$.

79. D: The 8 is in the tenths place, the 6 in the hundredths place, and the 7 in the thousandths place. Thus, 0.867 is equal to the sum of the product of 8 and $\frac{1}{10}$, the product of 6 and $\frac{1}{100}$, and the product of 7 and $\frac{1}{1{,}000}$.

80. D: The rectangular array represents the product of the side lengths of 7 and $(4 + 2)$, resulting in the expression $7 \times (4 + 2)$.

81. C: The probability may be written as $P(M \text{ or } G) = P(M) + P(G) - P(M \text{ and } G)$. Substituting the probabilities yields $P(M \text{ or } G) = \frac{4{,}985}{10{,}079} + \frac{4{,}113}{10{,}079} - \frac{2{,}045}{10{,}079}$, which simplifies to $P(M \text{ or } G) = \frac{7{,}053}{10{,}079}$, or approximately 70%.

82. D: The probability may be written as $P(N \text{ and } T) = P(N) \times P(T)$. Substituting the probability of each event gives $(N \text{ and } T) = \frac{1}{6} \times \frac{1}{2}$, which simplifies to $\frac{1}{12}$.

83. A: The slope of the graphed line is $\frac{1}{2}$. A line parallel to this one will also have a slope of $\frac{1}{2}$. Substituting the slope and the x- and y-values from the point $(-2,2)$ into the slope-intercept form of an equation gives: $2 = \frac{1}{2}(-2) + b$, which simplifies to $2 = -1 + b$. Adding 1 to both sides of the equation gives $b = 3$; therefore, the equation of a line that is parallel to this one and that passes through the point $(-2,2)$ is $y = \frac{1}{2}x + 3$.

84. B: Educators can encourage the student who both loves animals and excels in mathematics and sciences to consider a career as a veterinarian, a medical doctor requiring more education and training than physicians treating humans; the student who hates these subjects but excels at gentle handling and beautification (a) to consider a professional pet groomer career; the average math and science student who excels at rescuing and nursing animals (c) to consider working as a veterinary technician or in an animal rescue organization; the student concerned with wildlife conservation, protecting endangered species, and working to improve captive animal habitats (d) to consider becoming a wildlife biologist or zoo curator. Students may share a common interest, but need educator help relating it to different individual higher education and career decisions.

85. C: The theoretical probability is $\frac{1}{2}$, and $\frac{1}{2}(250) = 125$.

86. A: This graph shows a slope of 3, a y-intercept of –6, and the correct shading above the line. Using the test point (0,0), the equation $0 \geq 0 - 6$ may be written. Since $0 \geq -6$, the solution is the shaded area above the line, which contains the point (0,0).

87. D: If the learning objective states that students should use proportional relationships, it would be important for them to be able to express the proportion they are using. The teacher suggested 1 foot : 1 inch (or 1 : 12) but did not express it mathematically.

88. A: The situation may be modeled by the inequality $3x + 2y \geq 20$. Isolating the y-term gives $2y \geq -3x + 20$. Solving for y gives $y \geq -\frac{3}{2}x + 10$. Thus, the y-intercept will be 10, the line will be solid, the slope will be $-\frac{3}{2}$, and the shading should occur above the line because y is greater than or equal to the expression on the other side of the inequality.

89. D: The percent change can be found using the following formula.

$$\% \text{ Change} = \frac{\text{new} - \text{old}}{\text{old}} \times 100$$

The old value is his current rent (750), and the new value is his new monthly rent (900).

$$\% \text{ Change} = \frac{900 - 750}{750} \times 100$$
$$\% \text{ Change} = \frac{150}{750} \times 100$$
$$\% \text{ Change} = \frac{1}{5} \times 100$$
$$\% \text{ Change} = 20$$

Since the percent change is positive, this represents a percent increase of 20%.

90. B: The number of ways the letters can be arranged may be represented as $\frac{5!}{2!1!1!1!}$, which equals 60.

91. C: The amount he saves is equal to $0.1 \times \$2{,}450$. Thus, he saves $245.

92. C: The larger triangle has a base length of 6 units and a height of 6 units. The smaller triangle has a base length of 3 units and a height of 3 units. Thus, the dimensions of the larger triangle were multiplied by a scale factor of $\frac{1}{2}$.

93. C: The size of the sample space is the number of possible outcomes for one coin toss, 2, raised to the power of the number of coin tosses, 5. There are $2^5 = 32$ possible outcomes.

94. B: The points may be entered into a graphing calculator or Excel spreadsheet to find the least-squares regression line. This line is approximately $y = 1.67x + 1.74$. Substituting 15 for x gives $y = 1.67(15) + 1.74$, or $y = 26.79$. Thus, $27 is a good estimate for the profit received for selling 15 items. If a line of best fit is predicted visually, the slope between points near that line is approximately $1\frac{3}{4}$, and the line passes near the origin. This gives an estimate of $27.75, which is closer to $27 than any of the other choices.

95. B: If the statement is written in the form $p \to q$, then the contrapositive is represented as $\neg q \to \neg p$. Thus, the contrapositive should read, "If Bryan does not have an allergic reaction, he does not eat peanuts."

96. C: Allowing students time at the end of class to organize and secure their belongings is a great way to teach and model proper organizational skills for students. By allowing time at the end of class to secure their belongings and update their planners with important information, this teacher is emphasizing to her students how important it is to both organize and keep track of dates and responsibilities. This should help set a good foundation for the students to implement these skills in other classes so that they have the tools to be successful in school.

97. C: The original price may be represented by the equation $24{,}210 = x - 0.10x$ or $24{,}210 = 0.9x$. Dividing both sides of the equation by 0.9 gives $x = 26{,}900$.

98. D: Let $P(T)$ represent the probability of getting tails on the coin toss. We can see that $P(T) = \frac{1}{2}$. Let $P(P)$ be the chance of getting a prime number on the die. Of the possible outcomes (1 through 6), three are prime (2, 3, and 5), so $P(P) = \frac{3}{6} = \frac{1}{2}$.

Since $P(P)$ and $P(T)$ are not mutually exclusive, $P(P \text{ or } T) = P(P) + P(T) - P(P \text{ and } T)$. Because the events are independent, $P(P \text{ and } T) = P(P) \times P(T)$. Substituting the probability of each event gives $P(P \text{ or } T) = \frac{1}{2} + \frac{1}{2} - \left(\frac{1}{2} \times \frac{1}{2}\right) = \frac{1}{2} + \frac{1}{2} - \frac{1}{4} = \frac{3}{4}$.

99. B: The additive inverse property states that the sum of a number and its negative value is 0.

100. B: The slope may be written as $m = \frac{8-5}{0-5}$, which simplifies to $m = -\frac{3}{5}$.

Constructed Response

1. Part A: First, according to the problem, *m* is the value of the motorcycle after its initial depreciation. The value drops by 20%, so:

$$m = \$9{,}800 - (0.2) \times (\$9{,}800) = \$7{,}840$$

Using this value for *c* and substituting it in, the value formula then becomes:

$$y = \$7{,}840 - (0.08) \times (\$7{,}840) \times (x)$$

Finally, solve for *y* when $x = 4$:

$$y = \$7{,}840 - (0.08) \times (\$7{,}840) \times (4)$$
$$y = \$7{,}840 - \$2{,}508.80$$
$$y = \$5{,}331.20$$

Part B: The graph of *y* will be linear since *x* is raised to the first power. Reordering the function to the $y = mx + b$ format, the *y*-intercept and slope are readily identifiable:

$$y = \$7{,}840 - \left(\frac{\$627.20}{year}\right) \times (x)$$
$$y = -\left(\frac{\$627.20}{year}\right) \times (x) + \$7{,}840$$

Thus, the slope is $-\$627.20$ per year and the y-intercept is \$7,840. Plotting this function looks like the following.

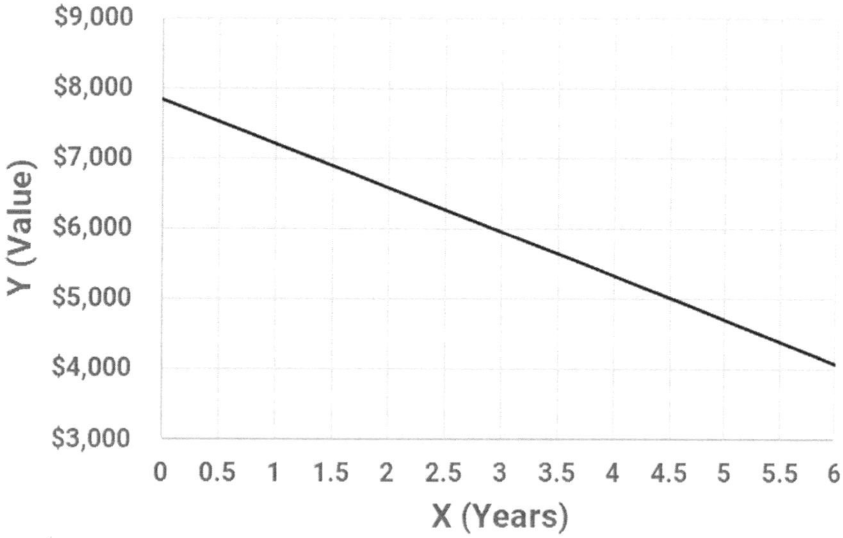

Part C: Using the axis values, it is readily apparent that the value function approaches \$6,000 when x is around **3 years**.

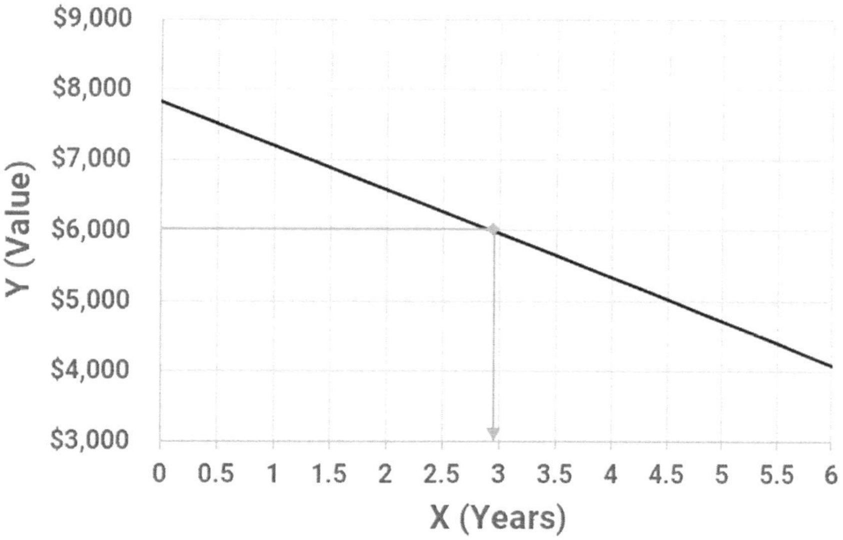

Part D: The way to use the function to find when the value is \$6,000 is to substitute it in for y and solve for x:

$$\$6{,}000 = \$7{,}840 - \left(\frac{\$627.20}{year}\right) \times (x)$$

$$-\$1{,}840 = -\left(\frac{\$627.2}{year}\right) \times (x)$$

$$\frac{-\$1{,}840}{-\left(\frac{\$627.20}{year}\right)} = x$$

$$x = 2.934 \text{ years}$$

After rounding to the tenths place: $x = 2.9$ years

2. Part A: The illuminated area is the area of the 9 circles. The 8 circles on the border are all the same size. We can find their area by first finding the radius. Since the diameter is 12 feet, the radius is $\frac{12}{2} = 6$ feet. Thus, the area for the outer lights is given by:

$$A = 8 \times \pi \times r^2$$
$$A \cong 8 \times 3.14 \times (6 \text{ ft})^2$$
$$A \cong 904.32 \text{ ft}^2$$

Now we find the area of the larger interior circle. The diameter is 15 feet, so the radius is $\frac{15}{2} = 7.5$ feet. Thus, the area is:

$$A \cong 3.14 \times (7.5 \text{ ft})^2$$
$$A \cong 176.63 \text{ ft}^2$$

Finally, we add the areas of the 8 smaller circles to the area of the larger circle to get the total illuminated area:

$$A \cong 904.32 \text{ ft}^2 + 176.63 \text{ ft}^2$$
$$A \cong 1{,}080.95 \text{ ft}^2$$

Part B: To find the area that will not be illuminated, we need to find the total area of the square and subtract the illuminated areas (found in part A). First, we need to find the length of the sides of the square. We know that the diagonal is 80 feet and that drawing the diagonal across the square splits it into two 45-45-90 triangles:

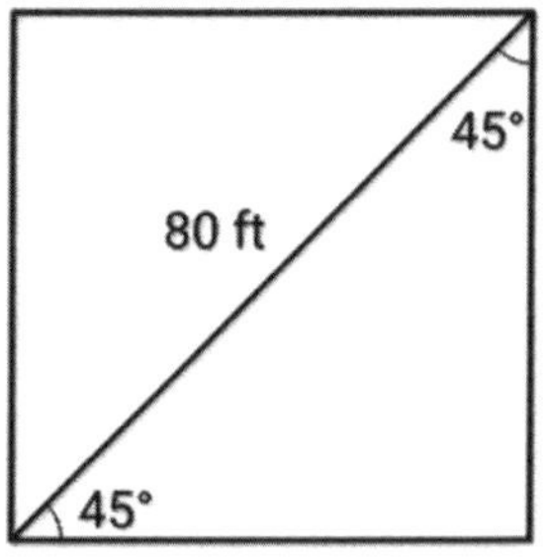

If we know the hypotenuse of a 45-45-90 triangle, we can find the legs by dividing by $\sqrt{2}$, so $\frac{80}{\sqrt{2}} \cong 56.57$ feet. Now we can find the area of the square:

$$A_{square} = s^2 \cong (56.57\text{ ft})^2 \cong 3{,}200.16\text{ ft}^2$$

Now we can subtract the illuminated area from the total square area to find the non-illuminated area:

$$A_{non-illuminated} \cong 3{,}200.16\text{ ft}^2 - 1{,}080.95\text{ ft}^2 \cong 2{,}119.21\text{ ft}^2$$

The percent area is found by:

$$\frac{A_{non-illuminated}}{A_{square}} \times 100\% = \frac{2{,}119.21\text{ ft}^2}{3{,}200.16\text{ ft}^2} \times 100\% \cong 66.22\%$$

Part C: It can be assumed that a ball would have an equal chance of landing anywhere in the area of the square. Thus, the probability it will land in an illuminated area is given by:

$$P_{illuminated} = \frac{A_{illuminated}}{A_{square}} \cong \frac{1{,}080.95\text{ ft}^2}{3{,}200.16\text{ ft}^2} \cong 0.338$$

3. Part A: The median of a list of values is the centermost value of an ordered list. If the ordered list has an even number of members, then the median is the average of the two centermost values. The two center values in this list are 83 and 86, so we add them and divide by 2 to find the median. The range of a list is the difference of the highest value and the lowest value. Thus, for this problem, the median is $\frac{83+86}{2}$ =84.5 and the range is $99 - 63 = 36$.

Part B: The stem and leaf plot would look like this:

Stem	Leaf
6	3
7	1 5 8 8
8	0 2 3 3 6 7 9 9
9	1 1 3 4 9

Part C: The mean of a list of values is the sum of all the members of the list divided by the number of members in the list:

$$\text{mean} = \frac{63 + 71 + 75 + 2(78) + 80 + 82 + 2(83) + 86 + 87 + 2(89) + 91 + 91 + 93 + 94 + 99}{18}$$

$$\text{mean} = 84$$